SURVIVING SOUTHAMPTON

Women, Gender, and Sexuality in American History

Editorial Advisors:
Susan K. Cahn
Wanda A. Hendricks
Deborah Gray White
Anne Firor Scott, Founding Editor Emerita

A list of books in the series appears at the end of this book.

SURVIVING SOUTHAMPTON

AFRICAN AMERICAN WOMEN AND RESISTANCE IN NAT TURNER'S COMMUNITY

VANESSA M. HOLDEN

UNIVERSITY OF ILLINOIS PRESS
Urbana, Chicago, and Springfield

Library of Congress Control Number: 2021935901
ISBN 978-0-252-04386-4 (hardcover)
ISBN 978-0-252-08585-7 (paperback)
ISBN 978-0-252-05276-7 (e-book)

Chapter 4 is derived in part from an article published
in *Slavery and Abolition* 38, no. 4 (2017), 673–696,
© 2017 Taylor & Francis, available online: http://
www.tandfonline.com/doi/full/10.1080/014403
9X.2017.1304612.

For Gram and Abuelita, my great-grandmothers.
Your memory is a legacy.
Your example of survival taught me to trust silence.
Your life stories taught me to persevere.

Contents

Acknowledgments

This book began with a question I asked as an eager undergraduate history student: "How did Nat Turner survive for months and evade capture after the Southampton Rebellion?" That question became my senior honor's thesis at Randolph-Macon Woman's College (now Randolph College). Nearly fifteen years of work later, what began as a question about enslaved women and their inexplicable absence from the narrative of America's most famous slave rebellion is now a book that centers community, resistance, and survival.

The mentoring I received as an undergraduate at Randolph-Macon Woman's College prepared me for graduate study and encouraged me to think like a scholar. Mara Amster, Heidi Kunz, and Julio Rodriguez each had an immeasurable impact on my development as a thinker and writer. John D'Entremont's mentoring and enthusiasm for my work helped me to proudly pursue a career as a professional historian.

In my time at Rutgers University, an entire network of scholars embraced me, supported my development as a scholar, and mentored me. I am grateful to Carolyn Brown, Indrani Chatterje, Dorothy Sue Cobble, Ann Fabian, Nikol Alexander-Floyd, Marisa Fuentes, Ann Gordon, Alison Isenberg, Temma Kaplan, Julie Livingston, Beryl Satter, and Camilla Townsend. Each took great care at different moments in my graduate career to support and mentor me, and each shaped my scholarly trajectory. Nancy Hewitt taught and continues to teach me lessons about who I want to be as a scholar. She was like a bonus adviser who always had time for me and contributed to my metamorphosis from student to scholar. Suzanne Lebsock, my adviser, taught me to find women's lives in Virginia's archives, to account for space and place, and to consider all of the ways my historical subjects were connected in antebellum Southampton County. She challenged me and guided my methodology. Deborah Gray White, also my adviser, became the coach who got me to the finish line in grad school. Her encouragement, sharp editorial eye, and instruction to persist, "bird by bird," bolstered my resolve and continues to serve as a model for mentoring in my life as a scholar and a faculty member.

The Virginia Historical Society, now the Virginia Museum of History & Culture, awarded me an Andrew W. Mellon Foundation Research Fellowship to work in their archives. Their archives expanded how I could cover enslaved and free Black children, and their staff provided invaluable assistance. The Library of Virginia and its librarians also offered me assistance and support at many stages of my research.

A number of colleagues at both Michigan State University and the University of Kentucky have helped me on my journey with this project. At Michigan State, Emily Conroy-Krutz, Pero Dagbovie, Denise Demetriou, LaShawn Harris, and Leslie Moch offered help, friendship, and support and continue to do so. Anastasia Curwood, Amy Murrell Taylor, and Karen Petrone eased my transition to a new institution as I wrapped up the project and have graciously spent time mentoring me and engaging with my work. Their help and friendship have made it possible for me to thrive at the University of Kentucky and to finish this project. Joe Clark, Phil Harling, DaMaris Hill, Kathi Kern, Kathryn Newfont, Melynda Price, Gerald Smith, Derrick White, and George Wright have all had a huge impact on my time at UK and are important supporters of my scholarship.

I am indebted to many mentors and friends in the field of Black women's history. Thavolia Glymph, Leslie Harris, Darlene Clark Hine, Tera Hunter, Jennifer Morgan, and Stephanie Smallwood have all engaged with me and my work, providing valuable insights and suggestions at professional meetings, seminars, and panels. I am forever grateful to Daina Ramey Berry and Erica Armstrong Dunbar for shaping my thinking and bolstering my resolve to finish writing this book. I also thank Amrita Chakrabarti Myers, Deirdre Cooper Owens, and Tamika Nunley for reading chapter drafts, laughing with me, and giving of their time to help me shape this work. Special thanks to Sally Hadden for her thoughtful reading and help with antebellum legal history.

From the start, Dawn Durante has stood by me and this project. She has worked through numerous drafts, crafted excellent suggestions, and stayed with me through various life changes. Her brilliance and kindness as an editor have saved this project more than once. I am so grateful that we got to work together at the University of Illinois Press.

I also thank Allison Miller and Rebecca Tuuri for their insistence that I do my work and put it out into the world. Conversations with John Adams, Robin Chapdelaine, Chris Mitchel, Svanur Pétursson, and Sara Rzeszutek have always lifted my spirits and pushed me forward. Kelly Dittmar's support has known no bounds. Kate Scott helped me through the final writing stages of the dissertation and continues to encourage me. Wendy Christopher offered patient advice that still guides me. I thank Yomaira Figueroa-Vásquez, Tacuma Peters, Tamara Butler, and Delia Fernandez for being my crew and Tanisha Ford and Treva Lindsey for their kindness and friendship. Jessica Marie Johnson has been my trench buddy and co-friendspirator; I am so honored to do this work with her.

My family and my kin have made my work possible. My parents, Jeff and Shelly, encouraged me to read and ask questions from an early age. They taught me to respect education and to challenge narratives. They raised me to find and tell the truth. Bryce and Doug, my first friends and my two-man cheering squad, I am so lucky to have brothers like you who support me and love me without condition. Jessica Eckman and Liz Latty, chosen cousins, you are the models of kin I strive to imitate. Clare Rittschof, my steadfast friend, thank you for getting me to go outside. Karen Marcus, thank you for encouraging me to write and live in truth. Camille Dungy, there is no way to capture how our friendship has shaped me and made me glad. Callie Violet, this project is only a little older than you are and being your godmother has grounded me. I am proud to be your Auntie V.

Mariama, your practice as a writer inspires me. Your presence as a voice of reason and calm has kept me. This life with you and Sir Henry sustains me. Thank you, love. Thank you.

Author's Note on Language and Sources

Writing the history of Black Virginians requires the use of archival materials and transcriptions of oral histories that reflect the racist attitudes of the people who produced them and the racial terms and language of the times. Reproducing, quoting, and citing these sources necessarily runs the risk of reifying dehumanizing violence against Black people and white denial of Black people's humanity. I have taken great care in choosing my words, selecting direct quotations, and attending to this possibility. But intent does not mitigate impact. The sources and their creators are not perfect. In a book about violence and resistance, I've cultivated an ethic of care that considers the impact of historical terms and language.

The Indigenous people whose lands the English encroached upon and called Southampton County call themselves Cheroenhaka. In their writings, they name themselves Cheroenhaka (Nottoway). As one chief notes, the name "Nottoway" is an anglicized version of a name their Algonquin-speaking neighbors gave them that they consider derogatory. I've used the name Cheroenhaka (Nottoway) out of respect for Southampton's first peoples, who remain to this day in the county.[1] When I refer to Indigenous people's lands, I call them Indigenous lands. When I refer to the specific reservation created by treaty between the Cheroenhaka (Nottoway) and the English in Southampton County, Virginia, I call it Indian Land.[2]

Whenever possible, I followed a guide P. Gabrielle Forman organized in collaboration with senior slavery scholars titled "Writing about Slavery? Teaching about Slavery?"[3] I use the terms enslaved person and enslaver instead of "slave" or "master/mistress." Enslaving African Americans required intentional action on the part of white men and women. Daily they chose to violently enforce race-based chattel slavery. Enslaved people is a term that recognizes the humanity of the Black people who are central to this project. In the case of indenture contracts and apprenticeships of children, I use the terms "master" and "mistress" because that was the language of legal guardianship, exploitative as it was, in the period. I do not use the N-word in my writing and edit it as "n——" in direct quotes.

I've chosen to transcribe direct quotes from the Slave Narrative Project of the 1930s Works Progress Administration exactly as they appear in the original sources. The voices of the formerly enslaved people who contributed to the narratives from Virginia have been filtered and changed enough by scholars and researchers. I've chosen not to add another layer of mediation to their interviews.

The Southampton Rebellion is a very famous and well historicized event in U.S. and African American History. I've consulted edited source collections, published transcriptions of primary materials, microfilmed primary documents, and original archival sources. In the interest of transparency, I've noted exactly which sources I've consulted in each note. For example, I looked at Southampton County court records. I've consulted Henry Irving Tragle's mid-twentieth-century published transcriptions, microfilm of the original minute books, and images of the original minute books housed in Southampton County. When I've looked at more than one version of the same source, I noted both in an endnote. I consulted different editions of *Weevils in the Wheat*, a collection of transcribed WPA narratives from Virginia. I note which edition I consulted in each instance. It is hard not to retrace other historians' steps when looking at such an important event. It is important to me that I account for all of the sources I've made use of in completing this work.

SURVIVING SOUTHAMPTON

Prologue

In the summer of 1937, in his interview with Susie R. C. Byrd, a worker with the Works Progress Administration (WPA), Allen Crawford stated, "I was bred and born and reared within three miles of Nat Turner's insurrection—Travis Place."[1] The interview documents Crawford's recollections of the stories he'd heard growing up in Southampton County about the Southampton Rebellion. Workers asked all participants in Virginia's WPA interviews about slave rebellions as a part of their official questions and were met with varying responses from interviewees.[2] Crawford's narration provides his recollection of the rebellion, its white and Black victims, and his own relatives who survived in its aftermath. Crawford's memories of his enslaved boyhood in Southampton are memories of the rebellion's impact well after the events of August 21–23, 1831, a testimony to his community's endurance. His memory of the stories his family passed down demonstrates how Black people remembered enslaved people's culture of resistance and survival in Southampton.

As a young boy growing up among adults who had survived the violence, the white rage, and the instability of Southampton County after the rebellion, Allen Crawford learned from an older generation what they thought was most important to pass on about the rebellion. Instead of recounting the heroic acts of Nat Turner or the violence of the enslaved men who followed him, Crawford's account focuses on another group of adults: enslaved women. For him, the story of the rebellion was not a story of visitors, men traveling from farm to farm to murder white enslavers, but a story of the visited, those enslaved people who remained after rebels came and went.

When asked, Crawford recalled what his elders had told him about the rebellion's aftermath. He recounted that when a local hunter found and captured Nat Turner, his captors stopped by the Edwards farm. Crawford's grandmother lived there at the time and saw Turner on his way to jail. Crawford remembered, "Grandma ran out an' struck Nat in the mouth, knocking the blood out and asked him, 'Why did you take my son away?'"[3]

Surviving Southampton: African American Resistance and Survival in Nat Turner's Community endeavors to explain the space between Crawford's grandmother's hand and Nat Turner's face. It is not about Nat Turner but about the community that produced him and the Southampton Rebellion. It begins with enslaved women, like Crawford's grandmother, who inhabited the county before, during, and after the rebellion took place. It attends to their community-constituted practices of resistance and survival.

Allen Crawford, alive in the 1930s having weathered slavery and emancipation, was his grandmother's legacy. Her story, with all of its grief and gumption, was what he passed on when he was asked to tell about the rebellion. Nat Turner is the man his grandmother hit so hard he bled. Discovering how women and their community survived to raise children who remembered and heeded their warnings and teachings about resistance is at the center of this book.

Introduction

An Intimate Rebellion

On the morning of August 22, 1831, after an evening of barbecue and spirits, a group of enslaved African American men started what would become the most famous slave rebellion in American history. The killing at the first house took no time at all. In those early hours, violence was the easiest part of the plan for the six enslaved men who began the Southampton Rebellion. Their biggest challenge was the climb through an upstairs window that one man had made so he could let the small group of insurgents in through the front door of the house. The man would have been familiar to the Travis family had there been light enough to see him. Had they had time enough to face the group who entered their home, the small family of whites would have recognized most of the men present. Joseph Travis, the farm's owner, had acquired through marriage to his wife Sally oversight of two of the men who entered his bedroom that evening. Putnam Moore, Sally's son from a previous marriage, was to inherit the enslaved property of his late father upon reaching maturity. Included in Moore's inheritance was Nat Turner, who would quickly become Southampton County's most famous enslaved resident. The band of enslaved men—Nat Turner, Will, Hark, Sam, Jack, and Henry—kept their vow to kill all whites, including women and children. They murdered the Travis family as they slept. After a failed attempt by Nat Turner to draw the first blood, Will's axe made quick work of each skull.[1]

It was still before sunrise when the men prepared to leave. It was then that Sam remembered that they had all overlooked one of the members of the Travis family as they hurried out to drill with the weapons they had commandeered at the Travis place. In the dark, amid the blood and carnage, they had forgotten to see to the Travises' infant. Henry and Will went back and murdered the child in its cradle. The enslaved men were determined that no one would inherit them.[2]

Over two days, August 22–23, 1831, the group of men grew from six to as many as fifty, though rumor would travel that hundreds of enslaved people had risen up in Southampton (see map 1). They moved from farm to farm in the neighborhood, seizing weapons and gathering information, vittles, and new recruits. Some of those recruits were not yet men. Boys and youths whom the rebels took up as they went along were so privy to the violence that whites would later use their testimonies to reconstruct the events of the rebellion. Rebels attempted to march on Jerusalem, the county seat across the Nottoway River from their neighborhood. But before they could cross, local militia met and challenged them. The rebels' failure to successfully cross Cypress Bridge ultimately signaled the decline of their forces.

By midday on August 23, local militia had disbanded the rebels, who had been unable to retain sufficient numbers overnight. Nat Turner disappeared and remained missing for two and a half months after the rebellion, hiding out near the Travis farm where his murdered enslavers once lived. A white neighbor who was out on a hunt captured Turner at the end of October. A local court tried him in Jerusalem and sentenced him to death. The local sheriff executed him on November 11, 1831. In all, the rebels visited at least fifteen residences and murdered fifty-five whites. Nearly half of those they killed were children.[3]

This narrative of events, one that closely mirrors what Nat Turner's jailhouse confessions reveal, features enslaved men and boys without connection to a community beyond each other. Turner is at the center of this narrative. His comrades in arms, a growing number of other enslaved men, appear in scant detail. But as Kenneth Greenberg notes in his introduction to his edition of Turner's jailhouse confession, the Southampton Rebellion was an intimate rebellion.[4] The rebels and their targets lived in close proximity. Racial hierarchy and the arduous labor demands of chattel slavery defined the thousands of daily interactions between Black people and

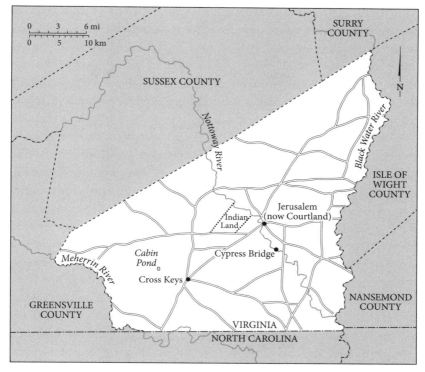

Map 1. Southampton County with key rebellion sites. Map by Bill Nelson.

whites. They all knew each other. Or, at least, whites assumed that they knew the people they enslaved. Conversely, Black peoples' familiarity with enslavers allowed for the swift success of the initial attack and those that followed.

Recently scholars have shifted the focus from "great male slave rebels" toward the enslaved communities that participated in and supported slave rebellions. Part of this historiographical shift has opened the door for an interpretation of enslaved people's resistance that includes African American women through the inclusion of everyday resistance on the part of African American communities. However, even though new critiques have challenged the centrality of individual male enslaved leaders and argued for the inclusion of women in a broader definition of enslaved people's resistance, violent rebellion remains the prerogative of enslaved men in the historiography. When historians finally include women in the discourse on

American slave rebellions and resistance, they do so not by framing them as co-conspirators in violent rebellion but as perpetrators of everyday resistance, a different type of rebellion. Thus, a gendered binary is developing in the scholarship: enslaved men rebel while enslaved women resist.

There were other rebellions and insurrections in North America, in the United States, and elsewhere in the Atlantic World.[5] Many were more extensively and better planned. Some included far larger numbers of enslaved people. And yet the Southampton Rebellion has a place of prominence in the historiography of both American and African American history. The success of Southampton's rebels in killing around sixty white men, women, and children was and still is remarkable. Whites thwarted other plots; they suppressed and put down other rebellions. But the Southampton Rebellion shocked a region that had been, at least outwardly, very confident in the merits of spreading slavery and shoring up the profitability of slavery as a social and economic system. Enslavers had accepted slavery's inherent security risks with heightened anxiety, entrusting militias and their own sense of mastery to protect them from enslaved people's rebellion and violence. One of the rebellion's lasting legacies is the debates it catalyzed in the halls of Virginia's legislature. That what began as a small group of enslaved men went on to force the question of slavery's viability in the Virginia General Assembly is significant not only in the history of the commonwealth but also in the political history of the nation.

The success of the Southampton Rebellion was the success of a community of African Americans. It was also the source of grief for that same community in the wake of rebellion events. Historians have come to call most American slave rebellions by the names of their leaders, a naming practice that obscures the communities in which each male leader was embedded. "Denmark Vesey's" rebellion, "Gabriel's" rebellion, and "Turner's" Rebellion are all names that hold up one man where whole neighborhoods and communities supported collective resistance and endured its consequences. Nat Turner is central to the historiography of American slave rebellion. Accordingly, inquiry into Turner's spirituality, psychological state, and biography dominate scholarship on the event that historians have come to call Turner's Rebellion. Understanding the community that produced the Southampton rebellion, a community that included African American women and children, opens up new possibilities for narrating the Southampton Rebellion. One of those possibilities is an explication of events that moves beyond resistance and rebellion toward understanding the community's survival praxis. The Southampton Rebellion, as I call it, was far bigger than one man's inspired bid for freedom. The Black communities of Southampton survived for generations afterward, both enduring and preserving the rebellion's legacy.

The historiography of Nat Turner has influenced most accounts of slave rebellion in the United States because of the rebellion's relative success and Nat Turner's place in American historical memory.[6] Most studies of American slave rebellions focus more on male leaders and on each rebellion's broader political significance than on the diversity of any rebellion's participants. Occasionally, historians cast the enslaved men involved in American rebellions as protectors of enslaved communities, grasping for masculine validation by protecting their wives, children, and kin. But communities were much more than the backdrops for resistive action; they were the genesis of resistive action. They were dynamic and diverse, and they were integral to a pervasive culture of resistance among African Americans.[7]

Stephanie M. H. Camp's work on enslaved women and resistance in the U.S. South stands alone in the field by fully exposing this hole in historical narratives; it challenges the centrality of armed rebellion in the historiography. She writes, "The valorization of the organized and the visible veils the lives of women, who rarely participated directly in slave rebellions and who made up only a small proportion of runaways to the North—the kinds of slave resistance that have been most studied within the United States."[8] However, although Camp's work does much to expand the definition of rebellion and resistance, women remain "everyday" resistors. Nevertheless, with Camp's important work in mind, it becomes clear that resistance and rebellion existed along a continuum that assumes that both men and women participated in strategies of both resistance and rebellion because of their connectedness within the enslaved community.

Scholars of America's slave revolts have largely espoused the view of enslaved women as simply excluded by enslaved men.[9] This makes little sense in light of African American women's integral role in the African American social and cultural communities, their ubiquitous resistive activity as described by Camp, and their often intimate, hardly consensual connection to white men and the white community.[10] The idea that enslaved people suddenly adhered to a gender code that made enslaved men more apt to rebel and able to exclude enslaved women from their plans is highly implausible in light of the historiography of African American women's history. African American women were involved in an active and constant culture of resistance among Black people. Their persistent everyday resistance positioned them within their communities to participate in moments of violent revolt.

The neighborhood where the Southampton Rebellion took place was also home to numerous sites of everyday resistance. Enslaved men were not the only members of the Black community who practiced everyday resistance. Free and enslaved adults and children moved through these sites of resistance throughout their workday. Much like physical geography, enslaved and free Black people experienced and constructed human geography, the mental mapping of both the physical location of humans and their social relationships in space and time, as a composite of many layers. To map the human geography of the many sites of resistance in Southampton County is to look beyond who the creators of the historical sources historians have associated with the rebellion mark as rebels—mostly enslaved men—and see the rebellion as a product of an interconnected community that includes enslaved women and children and free people of color.

Instead of presenting one new narration of the rebellion and the experience of community members, *Surviving Southampton* maps different communities into the resistive geography of Southampton County. Chapter 1, "Geographies of Surveillance and Control," begins with an exploration of the systems enslavers, landowners, and officials used throughout Virginia's history to attempt to control and constrain African American mobility. These geographies of surveillance and control were present on individual landholdings, in the neighborhood where the rebellion took place, and throughout the county. Whites did their best to extract labor from African Americans and police their movement to that end. Understanding the long history of surveillance allows for a deeper knowledge of the long history of African American evasion and resistance in Southampton County.

Chapter 2, "Enslaved Women and Strategies of Evasion and Resistance," uses the close study of one farm along the route of the rebellion and enslaved women who lived there to illustrate how enslaved women's labor afforded them greater mobility and an important role in building and defining geographies of evasion and resistance. Their daily movements mapped a resistive geography, evasion, and survival onto the spaces that whites meant to be sites of surveillance and control. During the rebellion, women passed information, provided food and sustenance, and were present during the violent murder of whites. Some chose to act in ways that whites would later read as rebellious while others remained circumspect. Their lives and experiences provide an alternate narrative of those who were the visited rather than the visitors on farms during the rebellion.

Chapter 3, "Free Issues: Free People of Color in Antebellum Southampton County," explores free women of color, who notably occupied a unique niche in the labor market in Southampton County. Free people of color were a definitive feature of Southampton's demography in the antebellum period. They constituted around 20 percent of the county's Black population. Very few free people of color owned their own land. The county's free Black community was not concentrated in an enclave. Rather, their high numbers attest to the frequency with which white farmers hired free Black laborers to supplement their labor needs. This was also true for enslavers and for farmers who did not enslave their laborers. Free people of color often lived alongside enslaved people and their material condition was often similar. Free women, whose work on small-to-midsized farms facilitated their place in community-constituted resistance, contributed to the survival strategies the community implemented after the Southampton Rebellion. Understanding the place of free people of color, particularly free women of color, in the county's labor economy is essential to understanding the fallout from the rebellion and the ways that free people of color contributed to strategies for survival in the broader African American community.

Chapter 4, "Generation, Resistance, and Survival: African American Children and the Southampton Rebellion," outlines the importance of children in Southampton's labor economy both as enslaved property and as indentured free workers. Black children and youths, both free and enslaved, appear throughout the official record of the Southampton Rebellion. Their mobility in and around Southampton figured into the rebels' strategy and recruitment practices. Black adults' responses to the violence of the event included both concern for their children and their use of children to spread word of the rebellion's events. The generational position of Black children as the community of the future was culturally significant and a pointed concern for African American adults, whose strategies for resistance and survival necessarily accounted for these children. Free and enslaved Black children and youths were a significant part of their community's strategies for resistance and survival. This chapter looks closely at the lives of five such children, four who were enslaved and one who was free, who appeared in court proceedings and were tried and convicted of participating in the rebellion. Adults intended to pass strategies of survival on to future generations. Recognizing the place of youths and children in community resistance provides a much richer picture of the rebellion as both gendered and generational.

Finally, chapter 5, "Surviving Southampton: Geographies of Survival," focuses on what the trial records for suspected rebels can tell us about Black resistive strategies after the rebellion. Typically, historians use trial records to reconstruct the events of the rebellion.[11] The trials were about mastery and about preserving the white-dominated social hierarchy. They were about reasserting power and making sure that the right sort of white men wielded it. The trials resulted in public executions and the removal of some enslaved men out of the state. Free people of color also went to jail, stood trial, and faced the gallows. The trial record also offers a view of how free and enslaved African American adults and children built evasive and resistive strategies even as whites wielded very real power over their lives. This localized legal context, one that was characterized by community relationships, allowed whites to build a condensed geography of surveillance and control in the county seat of Jerusalem. At the same time, African Americans mapped new geographies of evasion and resistance, just as they had in their own neighborhood. Through the court records this chapter traces resistive strategies as African Americans built them.

Beyond resistance, African Americans endeavored to endure in the wake of the rebellion. As Allen Crawford's narrative of that event reminds us, enslaved people continued to live, work, raise families, and grieve loved ones in the county after the chaos faded. His grandmother's story passed through generations. What Crawford recounted provides one glimpse of the fraught community in crisis that produced the rebellion and survived it. Survival was often a key component of resistance and resistive actions. The enslaved and free African Americans who lived in Southampton County were well aware that violent action against whites would most likely lead to death. Survivor is both a term for someone who has endured and our word for the bereaved. Southampton's Black communities remained to live and work among and around the empty space kin and community members left behind. Sowing death had reaped more death. Understanding the geography of loss by recovering the history of the community that produced the Southampton Rebellion is essential to understanding resistance and survival.

1

Geographies of Surveillance and Control

N——s was too smart fo' white folks to git
ketched. White folks was sharp too, but not
sharp enough to git by ole Nat.
—Cornelia Carney, formerly enslaved in
    Virginia, quoted in *Weevils in the Wheat*

A woodpile could be a place to lay low and avoid detection just as soon as it
could be the site of a beating. A kitchen could be a warm place to rest and
a site of abusive management by white enslavers. A field gang could slow
their progress between the same rows in which an enslaver extracted the
brutal labor of cotton culture from enslaved hands. Geographies of control
and resistance overlapped in antebellum Southampton County. Accessing
the lives of Southampton's enslaved population requires a different reading of available documentation. The voices of white interviewers, the court
clerk, enslavers, lawyers, the court, and local officials mediate most of the
appearances of enslaved women in the archive for the county during the
Southampton Rebellion. But their voices are still audible and legible. Accessing enslaved women's lives and experiences and those of the broader Black
community requires a close look at two key geographies: the geographies
of surveillance and control on small-to-midsized farms and geographies of
evasion and resistance.

Antebellum structures of surveillance and control had colonial roots in
the laws and customs of early Virginia. Southampton County, located in

Southside Virginia below the James River, belongs to some of the earliest parcels of Indigenous lands that Europeans colonized. White Virginians of all classes participated in establishing, maintaining, and enforcing the laws of the commonwealth. Within this broader structure of control, individual landowners cultivated their own geographies of surveillance and control on their own properties.[1] They administered punishments, oversaw enslaved people's labor, defined spaces on their farms, and decided who had access to those spaces. But white Virginians did not experience or define the social geography of the commonwealth on their own.

African Americans in antebellum Southampton County relied on generations of experience with white attempts to surveil them and control their daily activities when deciding when and how to resist. Understanding both the geography of the county and the longer history of disciplinary practices in Virginia and in Southampton County gives us a clearer view of how African Americans navigated geographies of evasion and resistance that layered on top of and beneath the county's physical, legal, and social geography. Enslaved and free Black Women were integral to the building of these networks, communities, and strategies of resistance over time. The community strategies Black people in Southampton used before the Southampton rebellion were essential to the knowledge base women used to make decisions about participating during the rebellion.

Geographies of Surveillance and Control

The environment of Southampton had considerable influence on the daily lives of residents. The physical geography of Southampton County dictated which crops were suitable and what type of labor was needed to cultivate those crops. Southampton County is swampy and hot. The Great Dismal Swamp lies about 20 miles to the east in what was then Nansemond County. Southampton is dotted with smaller swamps and ponds of its own. To the north and east, Sussex, Surry, Isle of Wight, and parts of Nansemond Counties cut Southampton County off from the James River, one of Virginia's most active waterways, and isolated it from Virginia's Tidewater region (see map 2). Southampton is one of Virginia's Southside counties. Greensville County lies to the west, and North Carolina is at the county's southern border. Southampton's most prominent waterway, the Nottoway River,

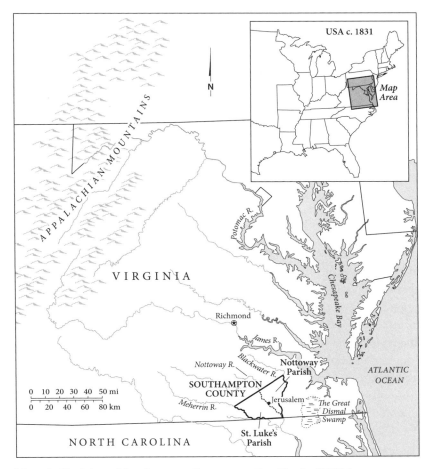

Map 2. Virginia and Southampton County, ca. 1831. Map by Bill Nelson.

bisects the county, and in the days before the arrival of railroads, it served as the county's link to its neighbors.

Originally, the Cheroenhaka (Nottoway), Iroquois speakers who lived among predominantly Algonquin-speaking neighbors, inhabited the land that became Southampton County.[2] In the 1600s, the Cheroenhaka (Nottoway) came into direct contact with Europeans when English colonizers arrived and began to push beyond the Blackwater River and deeper into Indigenous lands. Because of their cultural isolation, the Cheroenhaka

(Nottoway) quickly found themselves in the midst of a quandary that faced many Native American groups in whose lands bordered both the limits of European incursion and the lands of other Indigenous groups: should they forge alliances with other Native groups or enter into treaties with the European newcomers? Proximity to the violent colonial power struggle, a rapid depletion of their historic hunting grounds, and trade that resulted in debt to the new colonizers left the Cheroenhaka (Nottoway) with few options. In a series of negotiations, the English used treaties to take control over most Cheroenhaka (Nottoway) lands. By the eighteenth century, white officials had restricted the Cheroenhaka (Nottoway) to a reservation within English territory that had become a part of Isle of Wight County in the early 1700s. This arrangement was full of disadvantages for the Cheroenhaka (Nottoway), and their already small numbers declined. They remained into the early national period and still occupied a reservation recorded simply as Indian Land in the county in the 1830s. They remain a presence in Southampton County today.[3]

By the 1730s, the number of colonizers who had moved south and west from the Tidewater prompted officials to consider, and eventually create, a new county that divided Isle of Wight County. They called it Southampton County and established courts that first met there in 1748 and 1749.[4] The county established two major parishes in 1762 that were originally linked to Anglican congregations in the county and were later adopted as civil districts: Nottoway Parish, north of the Nottoway River, and St. Luke's Parish, on the river's south bank. Colonizers continued to journey to the county through the 1700s. Most of the newcomers endeavored to make a success of their landholdings by farming.

Along with its climate and swamps, Southampton County's most important natural feature was its sandy loam. This soil composition characterizes the northernmost tip of a band of soil that dips down through some of the best farmland in North Carolina and Georgia and into the Deep South. Despite the expectations of colonizers, this geological happenstance did not result in successful tobacco cultivation and Southampton's new residents had to try their hand at cultivating a range of crops.[5] By the 1820s and 1830s, landowners had experimented with and begun producing cotton both for their own use and as a cash crop. Cotton was an unusual cash-crop venture in Virginia, where tobacco had both reigned and waned in past generations. While cotton remained only one of the county's many crops, it was so labor intensive that it was a definitive part of the lives of many of the county's residents, especially its main labor force: enslaved people.[6]

The majority of enslavers in the neighborhood and the county were members of what could best be described as the middle class of the antebellum American South. They were stable but not fabulously wealthy. They were invested in slavery as a social and economic system, but most did not hold slaves in numbers that would qualify their agricultural operations as plantations.[7] They aspired to expand their cultivation of cash crops, but most could not support themselves without diversifying their agricultural production. All but the few large landholders of the county engaged in mixed agriculture to support themselves. Cotton was more common in Southampton County than anywhere else in Virginia, but it was not the county's king. Southampton was known less for its cotton yield than for its hogs and its orchards, from which farmers distilled fruit into brandy.

White migrants to the county brought enslaved laborers with them from the earliest days of the county. In the nineteenth century, Southampton was very much a slave society. By 1800, the enslaved population had outpaced the free white population and Southampton had become one of Virginia's majority Black counties.[8] Early in Virginia's history, lawmakers confirmed the absolute power over enslaved people's lives that their enslavers enjoyed. In 1669, Virginia law made it legal for an enslaver or their designated overseer to kill an enslaved person while correcting them.[9] Whites in Southampton County and all over Virginia constructed a number of systems for controlling enslaved people.

Enslavers used violence and brutality from slavery's inception to coerce labor from the enslaved, to discourage enslaved people from going truant or running away, and to prevent them from visiting violence and brutality upon whites in turn, but violence and brutality were limited preventative measures. Enslavers were most concerned with the amount of labor they could extract from enslaved people. They punished those whose behavior deprived them of this valuable labor, making an example of them with the intent of ensuring control over their enslaved labor force. Above all, white Virginians viewed the discipline of enslaved people to be the prerogative of individual enslavers. Their insistence on individual mastery left room for individuals to make human mistakes that enslaved people were keen to exploit.

The primary neighborhood from which enslaved rebels launched the Southampton Rebellion in 1831 lies in St. Luke's Parish. Sometimes called

Cross Keys after a central crossroads, the neighborhood had all of Southampton's defining features. St. Luke's was the swampier of the two parishes
in the county. Its white landholders owned more enslaved laborers than
those in Nottoway Parish. By the early antebellum period, they were farming cotton, a labor-intensive crop that in the 1810s-1830s proved incredibly
profitable elsewhere in the United States for those who were able to successfully produce it and bring it to market.

In those decades, the cotton frontier in the Old Southwest was rapidly
developing into the Deep South. Cotton, enslaved laborers, and the internal
slave trade would make fortunes for white Americans both in the region
and across the United States in the antebellum period. The Commonwealth
of Virginia supplied both white residents and staggering numbers of enslaved people to the substantial planter migration to the Deep South. But
Southampton County, which had soil that was hospitable to upland short-
staple cotton, remained a bit of an outlier. Some of the county's residents
did venture south and west. And some enslavers sold their human property
into the intrastate slave market. But those who remained and lived there
in the 1820s and 1830s belonged to a tight-knit, isolated community.

Legislators and local whites built and maintained geographies of surveillance and control throughout Virginia. At times, they used the physical
geography of the commonwealth. For example, colonial and state leaders
who were establishing state boundaries and borders, the officials who issued
deeds, recorded boundaries, and measured plots of land, and local courts
oversaw the deployment of local slave patrols. At all levels of government,
whites codified and institutionalized various practices and customs that
sought to control the movement of free and enslaved African Americans. As
Stephanie M. H. Camp writes, "Antebellum slaveholders put the principles
of restraint into practice in everyday life, adding to them their own plantation rules and building 'geographies of containment' on their farms."[10] What
Camp calls "geographies of containment" could also be called geographies
of surveillance and control. Whites of all classes in Southampton County
created and preserved geographies of surveillance and control meant to
exact mastery over the county's enslaved people and free people of color.

Enslavers and those who aspired to own human property took special care
to project confidence in white supremacy.[11] But their ability to manifest the
ideal of white patriarchal order in day-to-day interactions was not absolute.
At no time was this fact of daily life more galling than during moments of

acute crisis such as the Southampton Rebellion. Their geographies of surveillance and control were porous. Try as they might to control, surveil, and extract labor from enslaved and free Black people, whites had a tenuous and contested hold on power. Enslavers could exact oppressive labor regimes with their enslaved laborers under watchful eyes during daylight working hours. But when the workday was done, white enslavers could not be everywhere, and neither could the patrol system they built to control enslaved peoples' mobility once the sun was down. Local slave patrol records bear out this truth.

Slave patrol records in Southampton County exhibit trends that were present throughout Virginia in the antebellum period. Unlike some Atlantic World contexts, Virginia slave law did not come directly from England's other prominent slave societies.[12] Instead, white landholding Virginians tailored the commonwealth's geography of surveillance and control to the unique contexts and particularities of colonial Virginia. In early Tidewater Virginia, anxiety over the possibilities that indentured servants would escape and Indigenous people would attack, worries that white Virginians of all classes experienced, far outweighed concern over slave rebellion.

It was not clear to colonists in 1619, when the first enslaved Africans and Atlantic creoles arrived at Jamestown, Virginia, that enslaved workers would be their labor source of choice. In the early 1600s, the enslaved population of Virginia was relatively small and dispersed. People of African descent lived in the commonwealth as free, indentured, or enslaved people. They often worked alongside European and Indigenous indentured servants whose material condition was not noticeably different. The concerns of individual masters and enslavers about the retrieval of their laborers were much greater than the general white population's anxiety over possible rebellions. In this period of hybrid labor forces of free, enslaved, and indentured laborers, the onus of controlling the enslaved population fell on enslavers. Whites considered enslaved people to be their property and their responsibility.[13]

In 1695, Virginia elites designed a legal system to address the peculiar quandary crimes committed by human property presented. Virginians designed a specific legal system for matters that concerned enslaved people. Europeans imported Africans and Atlantic Creoles in increasing numbers in the latter part of the seventeenth century, and what had once been left largely to individual enslavers became a matter of community safety for European leaders and officials. Virginia's white colonists designed their legal system to preserve the status of enslaved people as property, protect the status of enslavers as free whites, and address crimes committed by enslaved people that affected the broader white communities in which they lived.[14] Laws for court proceedings and for legal precedent were dynamic mechanisms of power that were primarily concerned with the status of white men in relation to other residents in the community. It took Virginia's leaders generations to develop the law and the mechanisms to enforce it.[15]

Initially, the need to completely restrict the movement of enslaved people was not apparent to early Virginia enslavers or the greater white population.[16] It was not until the late seventeenth and early eighteenth centuries that European colonists' concerns with the rapidly expanding enslaved population began to overshadow the fears of previous generations that Indigenous people would attack and servants would revolt. After a rebellion in 1676, elite colonists became increasingly alarmed at the possibility that indentured servants and enslaved people could find common cause against them. The rebellion's leader, Nathaniel Bacon, was an elite European colonist. Virginia's leaders passed a succession of codes dictating assemblies of people of African descent, their ability to own weapons, punishment for their participation in insurrection, and restrictions on their mobility. European landowners began to leave behind the use of indentured laborers for Europe in favor of enslaving people of African descent.[17] In response, legislators codified a system of surveillance to thwart rebellion beyond enslavers' ordinary discipline, the intervention of local sheriffs and justices of the peace, and basic court proceedings that addressed grievances on an individual level.[18]

In practice, enslavers remained the primary arbiters of discipline and control in enslaved people's lives. Many enslavers in the seventeenth-century Tidewater needed mobile enslaved laborers to do necessary forms of labor. By the 1700s, the tobacco economy had resulted in a dramatic increase in the importation of enslaved Africans and Atlantic Creoles.[19] With the increase came new anxieties for the entire white population of colonial Virginia. Their solution—additional slave codes, a separate court system for enslaved people, and slave patrols—was born out of the fear of slave rebellion and not from the desire to limit enslaved people's movement for its own sake.[20]

Virginia's laws and customs continued to protect the social position of individual enslavers. The commonwealth's leaders developed strategies to

"paterrollers would whip you ef they caught you 'dout a pass. Ef you had a pass, didn't whip you—jes would git in touch wid you marster and tell him dat they had one of his n——s, de he'd let him go."[39] Even though patrols were given orders to turn all truants they encountered over to a local justice, enslaved people expected that patrols would punish them before returning them to their enslavers, a reality that was heightened during Crawford's post-rebellion childhood.

Being caught by a patrol was no light matter. Mrs. Fannie Berry remembered that brutality at the hands of patrollers caused one woman to commit suicide. Remembering a woman named Nellie, Mrs. Berry recounted that after being captured and beaten, "[Nellie] had tol' me day befo': 'Fannie, I don' had my las' whippin' I gwine to God.'" After hiding out in a haystack, Nellie sneaked out at night to a nearby hill and leaped to her death.[40] This final act of defiance deprived her enslaver of her labor and ended her suffering. Both men and women encountered patrollers, suffered brutality at their hands, and found ways to cope with their violence in both extreme and subtle ways.

It is not surprising that enslaved people's primary strategy for subverting the patrol system was to simply do their best to avoid the patrols entirely. Geographies of evasion included hiding places, routes for escaping detection or losing patrollers, and tactics to ensure that as many enslaved people as possible could escape the risk of brutality if they were caught by their enslaver or a patrol. Enslaved people would plan meetings on nights when they knew no patrol would ride out. They would pass word to one another that although a meeting would be held, the patrols were going to ride. This gave people the chance to decide if the risk was worth taking.

Women were important conduits of information about geographies of surveillance outside the bounds of farms. Mrs. Bird Walton remembers her mother receiving warning right under her enslaver's nose. While her mother worked in the kitchen alongside her female enslaver, Jerry, a footman, asked Mrs. Walton's mother, "Howdy, Mary, did you know dey was bugs in de wheat?" "Bugs in the wheat" or "weevils in the wheat" was a folk expression that was code for patrollers riding out. Mrs. Walton's mother decided not to attend an illicit party that night and her enslaver was none the wiser.[41] From her location in the farm's kitchen, her mother was also well positioned to pass the information she received from the house on to people she fed in the fields.

Throughout the antebellum period, some enslaved people chose to attend meetings and travel even though patrols were present, despite the white community's periodically heightened vigilance. Enslaved people developed strategies for hiding their meetings and knowing the whereabouts of patrols. As a general precaution, they posted lookouts and used pots around the meeting space to catch sound.[42] Lookouts ran as decoys, leading patrols into obstacles like brambles placed along the roadway or into rivers where they could be thrown from their horses.[43] Additionally, lookouts sometimes crippled the horses patrollers dismounted as they pursued truants or looked for meetings.[44] Each strategy was devised to help as many attendees avoid the patrol as possible; the logic was that while the patrols might catch some, they could not catch everyone.

Along with evasion techniques and the use of lookouts, African Americans relied on acts of spontaneous kindness and solidarity from other Black people. Not all who offered help to those who were avoiding the patrols planned on doing so. Mrs. Jennie Patterson remembered opening her cabin door to find a woman she did not recognize asking her, "Can I stay here all night?" The unnamed woman stayed in Mrs. Patterson's bed while she kept a lookout and watched as patrollers rode right past her cabin. "Next morning she stole out from dar, and I, Baby, ain' never seen her no more." Mrs. Patterson's careful watch denotes her caution just as her willingness to harbor a fugitive exemplifies how women contributed to broader geographies of evasion. Her bed was a resting place. Her cabin, on that night, was a safe harbor. "You see we never tole on each other," she noted.[45]

Women participated in the broader network of subversion and resistance outside their immediate farms as both truants and the support network that made truancy tenable. Lorenzo L. Ivy, another formerly enslaved person from Virginia, remembered accounts of his grandmother's frequent truancy in the woods near where she was enslaved. He also remembered how his mother offered his grandmother support: "My mamma say she used to always put out food fo' her an' she would slip up nights an' git it."[46] Women like Jennie Patterson and Lorenzo Ivy's mother actively sustained the support networks upon which truants relied. Their cabins, larders, and ration pokes were sites and objects of oppression that figured into their enslavers' geographies of surveillance and control. At the same time, they were also distinct features of geographies of evasion and resistance.

At times, enslaved people confronted whites directly. Evasion was not always possible, and enslaved people planned carefully for confrontation. For example, Betty Jones remembered how her community navigated being discovered by local patrols. "Dey had a big wooden log stuffed wid mud in de fire," she recalled. When patrollers arrived, two men shoveled the smoldering coals out the door of the cabin directly on the men outside. "Dey runned from de fire, an' we runed fom dem," she remembered, "Ain' nobody git caught dat time."[47] Perhaps her addition of the words "dat time" held other memories of less successful evasion tactics.

All over antebellum Virginia, enslaved women and free women of color were embedded in networks of evasion and resistance. They went truant and they helped truants. They absorbed information about local patrols and served as conduits of information. They were very aware of the dangerous intersection between the geography of surveillance and control their enslavers curated and the transgressive geography of evasion and resistance they built with other Black people.

Understanding the layered social and physical geography of slavery in Southampton and Virginia is important for understanding Black women's roles in the Southampton rebellion more broadly. Most remained firmly rooted to the farms where they labored as men visited rebellion on farm after farm late in the summer of 1831. Knowing whites' surveillance practices and attempts to control Black life in Southampton better contextualizes the geographies of the many small to midsized farms that dotted the majority of Southampton County in 1831. In the same way, knowing that the actions of enslaved and free Black women in the summer of 1831 were not spontaneous but were deeply rooted in long-standing strategies of evasion better explains their absence from some rebellion activities and their presence in others. Black women were both savvy and well positioned to process and disseminate intelligence while providing critical support to their communities. They did both during the Southampton Rebellion.

2

Enslaved Women and Strategies of Evasion and Resistance

Got to have good pickers fo' 'Ginny [Virginia]
cotton. Ole Marse would go down to Car 'lina
an' hire pickers to come an' help when he got
a good crop. We'd do some kind of pickin 'den.
No 'th Car 'lina n———s used to say dey could
outpick 'Ginny n———s, an' some of 'em could
too, but dey warn't many could outpick me.

—Miss Susan Mabry, born 1850,
  Southampton County, Virginia, quoted
  in *Weevils in the Wheat*

Charlotte and Ester

The heat of a Southside August was kind to cotton and nothing else. The
only other living things that looked forward to the heat were preachers; it
was sitting-in season for the white folk who could travel to revivals. They
would wait on the Lord and wait for the king, king cotton, to burst open,
make his presence known, and demand more tribute in sweat and scars. The
white fluffy wealth was all over the county. Some big men had vast fields,
while many others had patches here and there. In the heat and the foggy
haze of swampy humidity, the cotton no longer needed chopping. It just
needed sun and water and time. Then the hardest season would come in
a wave of bursting bolls. The cotton would open up and the hands would
sweep it up and the gins would clean it up and the hands would mote it out

and card it.[1] But in August, the cotton would bide time and mature and the hands would spend less time in the fields and more time occupied elsewhere.

For women like Charlotte, there was never an end to work, no matter what season it was. The cotton was just one thing growing. In the summer of 1831, for example, her new enslaver, Lavinia Francis, was close to welcoming her first child. Lavinia was only eighteen at the time. Her young husband, Nathaniel Francis, brought his wife to his childhood homeplace from Northampton County, North Carolina, just over the border from Southampton County, Virginia. Lavinia took over as manager of the farm's domestic labor and laborers from Nathaniel's mother, who still lived on the place. With the new woman of the house came another new woman. Ester, an enslaved woman, came along from North Carolina as a wedding gift like a trunk or a trousseau. The heat could not have been easy on Lavinia in her condition. She'd grown up in the heat of the region just across the border, but that summer she was sweating for two.

The Francis family perhaps later recalled rebels arriving on their place in the morning of August 22, 1831, on the heels of a young boy they knew from the farm of neighboring kin, but the truth was that rebels had arrived much earlier than that. Francis's enslaved laborers, Sam and Will, were both original conspirators with Nat Turner, who, along with a small group of others, had plotted at least since that spring to foment rebellion in the neighborhood. Will had been in the Francis holdings since the time of Nathaniel's father, Samuel Francis. The enslaved man Sam had arrived on the farm in the early 1820s. As one historian of the rebellion points out, "The holdings of Nathaniel and his sister together would produce four of the seven original insurgents, including the leader, his chief lieutenant, and the 'executioner.'"[2] Ultimately, six men and boys from Nathaniel Francis's place, none of whom were recent arrivals to his holdings, traveled the county with the rebels in August 1831.[3]

The happenings around and outside the Francis homeplace have received ample attention from historians. When the rebels arrived on the farm, they murdered the Francises' overseer and two white boys. They searched for Lavinia, Nathaniel, and Nathaniel's mother; when they could not find them, they went on to a neighboring farm. The rebellion at the Francis farm did not end when the men and boys left. Charlotte and Ester, who remained behind, set to work preparing food for the men to return to and began fighting over Lavinia's belongings. They assumed that rebels had murdered her.

Lavinia Francis was not dead. She'd passed out from the heat in an attic cubbyhole where a person enslaved by the extended Francis family had hidden her. When she woke up, she made her way to the kitchen behind the house, where she could hear Charlotte and Ester fighting. The three women regarded each other and the following moments moved quickly. Charlotte grabbed a handy knife and lunged at Lavinia. Ester stepped between them and held off Charlotte, who just missed dispatching their enslaver. Lavinia grabbed a nearby wheel of cheese and fled to the woods. In the space of a few hours, Lavinia Francis had escaped death twice, once at the hands of enslaved men and once at the other end of an enslaved woman's kitchen knife.[4]

Ester and Charlotte's participation in the Southampton Rebellion was distinctly different from that of their male counterparts, who were elsewhere in the county by the time Lavinia Francis came to. Past histories of the Southampton Rebellion regard Ester and Charlotte's story as anomalous and their actions as spontaneous. However, their motives were not different from those of male rebels. The two women acted no more out of personal resentment and frustration than the men for whom they cooked dinner. What happened in the Francis kitchen was as much a part of the Southampton Rebellion as Nat Turner's initial Cabin Pond meeting and the killing of Nathaniel Francis's kin in his front yard. The future rebels had lived on the place long before August of 1831. Including the enslaved women who lived on the farm in that category means that some rebels never really left.

However, their rebellion happened within the context of the Francis farm's specific geographies. The farm's kitchen was the site of significant domestic labor and a space where the Francises may have housed enslaved people. It was both intimate space and a thoroughfare. Within individual households and on individual farms, whites reproduced and curated the same geographies of surveillance and control that broader Virginian society maintained. Law and custom dictated that enslavers were the architects of control in intimate spaces, sites of domestic labor, spaces where enslaved people processed each season's yield, and the fields. Enslaved women's gendered labor forced them to navigate each type of space on small and medium-sized farms. The Francis kitchen was one such space, and Ester and Charlotte's confrontation with Lavinia Francis is one example of two geographies intersecting.

Versatile Laborers: Cotton, Mixed Agriculture, and Women's Labor

In the early antebellum period, the majority of farms in Southampton County were small and midsized agricultural operations. The county boasted a small number of established planter families, some of whom were descendants of the county's earliest founders and owned many acres and numerous enslaved laborers. But the majority of the population did not qualify as landed gentry, especially in the neighborhood that produced the Southampton Rebellion. For example, of the fifteen farms the rebels visited in the late summer of 1831, only one had an enslaved population of over 100.[5] Only three were home to thirty or more enslaved laborers. The remaining farms averaged about fifteen enslaved laborers each.

The primary neighborhood from and within which enslaved rebels launched the Southampton Rebellion in 1831 lies in St. Luke's Parish. The neighborhood had all of Southampton's defining features. The parish was the swampier of the two parishes in the county. Its white landholders owned more enslaved laborers than those in Nottoway Parish. Southampton's middling farmers needed more laborers than they could afford to purchase, as evidenced in the high number of free people of color who were hired and bound as supplemental labor throughout the county.[6] Instead of a community of landowners who found their soil and cash crop in decline, as was the case elsewhere in the commonwealth, Southampton's middling and wealthy agriculturalists found themselves on the northernmost boundary of a booming economy.

Gendered labor norms led enslavers to expect that enslaved women would be versatile laborers. Nathaniel Francis, who enslaved Ester and Charlotte, ran an established farm in the heart of St. Luke's Parish. His home was modest. The building itself, which had two rooms downstairs and a second floor that was little better than a loft, housed at least five people: Nathaniel Francis, his mother, their overseer, and Nathaniel's two orphaned nephews, both under the age of ten. His middling economic status and multigenerational household was typical of farms in the county. Nathaniel had done relatively well for himself. He could afford to marry Lavinia Hart in 1830. Her arrival on the Francis homeplace signaled the beginning of a family of his own, an important step for an aspiring community leader.[7]

Francis belonged to a significant kinship network. Nathaniel's brother, Salathiel, and sister, Sally, lived on nearby farms. Salathiel was attempting to make a small farm profitable with the help of a handful of enslaved people.[8] Sally had recently married Joseph Travis, a farmer and carriage maker. She brought into her new household her young son from her first marriage, Putnam Moore, and enslaved laborers from her first husband's holding. Putnam was expected to inherit his late father's human property upon reaching maturity. The inheritance he brought into the Travis household included the man who would soon become Southampton's most famous resident, Nat Turner.

Nathaniel Francis had a wealth of kinship and community ties but was by no means rich. Because Nathaniel had an overseer and Ester, an enslaved domestic, the community may have had the impression that his was a household on the rise. But the Francises were far from landed gentry. Nathaniel Francis's property holdings included fifteen enslaved people and six free people of color.[9] But the strength of his workforce cannot be determined by these raw numbers. Not all of these hired and enslaved laborers were old enough in 1830 to serve as full hands. Enslavers used the terms "full hand" and "half hand" to denote the labor expectation for individual enslaved people and their value in the marketplace. Only six of Nathaniel's enslaved laborers were adults capable of taking on the labor of full hands. The rest were youths and children who were able to pull the weight of half hands at best and were certainly still learning the skills needed to take on adult labor.[10]

Another thing that indicated Francis's financial status and agricultural goals was the fact that he employed three free adults of color, two men and one woman. Many householders in the county used free people of color as cost-effective supplementary labor. They could be expected to do the work of enslaved people, but they did not have white enslavers who were concerned with the well-being of their property, as was the case for hired slaves. The remaining free people of color on the Francis farm were children. On the eve of the Southampton Rebellion, Nathaniel had nine adult laborers to help bring in his cotton and tend to the other crops on his farm.

For women like Ester and Charlotte, work on the Francis farm was diverse. Five women—two white, two enslaved, and one free woman of color—performed all of the domestic labor and processing work for a farm of twenty-seven people. White women of Lavinia Francis's class were usually spared field labor, but they were expected to manage burgeoning domestic economies that required a significant amount of diligence. Lavinia would have overseen and participated in the preservation, preparation, and production of food. She would have managed and undertaken dairy work and animal husbandry alongside her mother-in-law. The enslaved women on the farm would have been expected to labor at the same domestic tasks when they could be spared from fieldwork and cotton processing. Lavinia would have overseen and worked beside them. As Nathaniel Francis's new wife, she would also have been responsible for seeing that the entire household was clothed and fed.[11]

As the women worked, children would have been frequently underfoot. The Francis farm was home to eleven children under 10 years old: Nathaniel's two nephews and nine African American children. Even if the latter were put to work around the age of 5, they still required supervision, most likely provided by the farm's women. And by the spring of 1831, Lavinia found herself pregnant with her and Nathaniel's first child. This would have altered the workload for the enslaved women who lived there and for the white women faced with the impending care of an infant.

On larger plantations throughout the antebellum South, skill level rather than gender often dictated what tasks an enslaver assigned their enslaved labor force.[12] Skill also dictated labor assignments on smaller farms. But with their smaller labor forces, gender also influenced the fluidity of task assignment. Fieldwork was one type of labor that separated enslaved women from white women and, to an extent, from free women of color. But it was not the only work enslaved women were expected to do for the good of the economic viability of small to medium-sized farms. Often historians note that very few enslaved women performed domestic labor for their enslavers, making the distinction between housework and field labor sharp and skewed toward a high ratio of field-workers.

On the large plantations of the American South, it was true that most enslaved people of both sexes performed field labor for their enslavers and enslaved women did domestic labor in their own communities. Broadly speaking, very few enslaved people across the South practiced skilled trades or performed domestic labor exclusively for their enslavers. Most white enslavers simply could not afford to keep enslaved people who did not perform fieldwork. The majority of Southampton's sites of enslavement were small or medium-sized farms, and the labor needs of each farm were not the same as those of large plantations. On farms of that size, the labor required of enslaved women changed with the agricultural cycle and included important roles both in fieldwork and in the domestic economy of each farm.

Enslaved women across the American South were involved in all of the many labor-intensive tasks of the cycle of cotton cultivation. Unlike modern crops shaped more by bioengineering in agricultural labs than by natural selection, antebellum crops varied greatly by region. Although Southside Virginia cotton was related to the upland cotton found in Louisiana or Georgia, it likely evolved along unique lines in response to environmental factors such as the climate, weather cycles, and insects of Virginia. According to enslaved people from the Southside, Virginia's "cotton plants was small and scrumy wid little buds."[13]

Smaller plants meant a longer chopping period. Chopping involved hoeing out competing crops that might overtake and shade growing cotton plants. Sticky cotton bolls meant more work that required greater skill at harvest time.[14] Harvesting the prickly bolls that grew to between knee and hip height was the most notoriously arduous task of the cotton-growing cycle. Enslaved laborers across the south needed expert dexterity to avoid slicing, cutting, and piercing their hands on cotton bolls as they moved through row after row. In Southampton, where the cotton bolls were "small an' scrummy an' stick to de plant like green bark," the harvest required particularly skilled hands.[15]

On larger plantations, the gang system, the practice of sending harvesters in groups organized by ability down rows, was the most favored system of labor organization. On smaller farms, a scaled-down version of this method of harvest was practiced and every available hand was used to harvest the cotton crop. Some farmers turned to hired labor in addition to their smaller enslaved labor forces.[16] The harvest started in September and sometimes ran as late as November. While these additional hands helped bring in the harvest in a timely manner, they did not alleviate the workload of female fieldhands.

Labor related to the cotton crop was not limited to fieldwork. Cotton required a number of intermediary processing steps: ginning, moting, carding, spinning, dyeing, weaving, cutting out garment pieces from patterns, and sewing. Processing work was considered women's and at times children's labor. The labor enslaved women performed daily that related to cotton put them in proximity to a number of spaces on each farm during and after the harvest. As a result, enslaved women had access to most farm residents. They were mobile within the landscape of a farm at any hour of the day.

While evidence for the specific cotton-processing tasks in Southampton is sparse, there is significant evidence throughout the cotton South for the role enslaved women played in processing cotton and other "slave crops." In Virginia, a state with a long tradition of tobacco culture, enslavers often delegated the steps that processed tobacco for market to enslaved women. Many descriptions of tobacco cultivation, including the testimonies of en-slaved people, specify that women completed the long processing phase of the tobacco growth cycle. Gabe Hunt, a formerly enslaved Virginian, remembered that "de women would take each leaf up an' fix de stem 'tween two pieces of board, den tie de ends together. Den hand'em all up in dat barn an' let it smoke two days an' two nights. Got to keep dat fire burnin' rain or shine, 'cause if it go out, it spile de tobaccy."[17]

Women were responsible for drying, curing, separating, grading, and packaging tobacco for market. Women's role in the processing of cash crops is also evidenced in other "slave crops." For example, women processed rice for market in South Carolina, pounding the grain just as their ancestors had before them in West Africa.[18] Women milled cane and distilled rum in the Caribbean.[19] And throughout the cotton South, women ginned, carded, and spun cotton. It is therefore reasonable to believe that enslaved women played a role in the processing of Southampton cotton for market.

Roller gins for removing the seeds from cotton were used in East and Central Asia and in Africa long before the Common Era. In 1794, Eli Whitney patented the saw gin, an improvement on an ancient design that used teeth to pull cotton fiber free of cottonseed. Whitney's invention most famously decreased the time it took to process raw cotton. The saw gin was much easier to use and required much less physical exertion. Unlike the large roller gins of the past that required prime (often male) hands to operate them successfully, the saw gin could be operated by enslaved women. However, ginning was only the first step in processing the raw fiber after harvest.

All available hands participated in moting, the removal by hand of seed particles left behind after ginning. Moting was the last processing step both men and women engaged in. Once enslaved laborers moted the harvest, they either packed the clean fiber for shipment to industrial centers in the northeastern United States and across the Atlantic or began the process of spinning cotton fiber into yarn. The evidence for Southampton County indicates that some of the county's cotton remained in Southampton for processing throughout the antebellum period and was processed by free and enslaved African American women in the county.[20] This processing work would have happened during the late autumn and winter months, occupying women long after the harvest was completed. Cotton processing produced the fiber that laborers eventually spun, wove, cut, and sewed into clothing. The production of clothing, even after the advent of factory-made pieces, was almost exclusively the domain of antebellum women, especially those who needed to clothe the people they enslaved.

Throughout the antebellum period, southern cotton farmers used home-spun material. While Whitney's famous cotton gin gave rise to the economic flourishing of the cotton South, the industrial technology that would transfer production of cotton textiles from home to factory did not develop until the 1810s.[21] Even after factory equipment began making yarn from American upland short-staple cotton in 1813, store-bought yarn was too expensive and was not widely used outside the Northeast until the 1830s. Even then, many southern planters continued to use homespun cloth to clothe their enslaved laborers.[22] Both white and Black women performed most of the labor needed to produce clothes from raw cotton. By the early antebellum years, spinning and weaving were considered to be women's work, as were cutting cloth and sewing garments.

Many other crops dictated the cycle of agriculture on most Southampton farms. Some, like corn or garden produce, had work cycles that could be interspersed between planting, chopping, and harvesting cotton. Hogs, Southampton's other major export, roamed area forests to forage for their own keep. They were slaughtered in late winter, well before planting season. However, harvesting the county's famous orchards, which produced apples for brandy, overlapped with the cotton harvest in the autumn. Other work performed exclusively by women—processing dairy products, doing laundry, and preserving and preparing food—posed constant labor demands that exclusively occupied Black and white women.

Enslaved women were uniquely placed to learn, move through, and act within the layered physical and social geographies of each farm. Their mobility and proximity to whites within the boundaries of each farm made them an invaluable resource in community strategies of resistance and survival. It is true that most slaves worked in fields all over the American South. On large plantations with wealthy owners, some enslaved people served exclusively in a domestic capacity. The split between the fields and the enslaver's house, yard, and outbuildings was sharper and more regimented and surveilled on large plantations. But owners of smaller farms had needs that required a more versatile use of the labor of the people they enslaved.

Instead of viewing the mobility of enslaved women as a threat, whites saw their versatility as an asset. Landowners with smaller enslaved labor forces, smaller acreages, and diversified crops to tend could not afford a strict division between the fields and the house, particularly for enslaved women and girls. Enslaved women could perform domestic tasks, agricultural processing work, and field labor. They crossed the imagined boundaries between field and house daily. It was crucial to production. While historians have often noted that enslaved men were the more mobile sex because of their (limited) access to skilled trades, gendered labor facilitated greater mobility for enslaved women on small to midsized farms.

The community that produced the Southampton Rebellion consisted primarily of farms that fit this profile. Women of African descent lived all over Southampton County. They outnumbered white women significantly in 1830. In the area where the rebellion occurred, enslaved women could be found on almost every farm. In the households the rebels visited on August 22 and 23, 1831, there were more than five times more enslaved women and girls than white women and girls. Enslaved women were the women of Southampton County, and their labor was essential to the county's economy.

Enslaved people extended their strategies of evasion and subversion into their laboring lives. Resistive practice had to be prudent and persistent. Enslaved people's many forms of everyday resistance involved finding ways of depriving white enslavers of their labor. Work stoppages, sabotage, feigned illness, and truancy all affected the production goals of whites. Work, labor regimes, agricultural cycles, and task assignments influenced how enslaved people plotted both open rebellion and day-to-day survival.

Charlotte and Ester were not the only enslaved women rooted to the geography of the farm where they labored during the rebellion. According to the extant records of the rebellion, most of the enslaved women were the visited rather than the visitors. While men traveled the neighborhood, women stayed put and served as the rebellion's intelligence network and supply line. Their experience and mobility as gendered laborers allowed them mobility and access within farms that perfectly positioned them for this role.

Lucy, an enslaved woman who lived and worked on the farm of John T. Barrow, became a rebel in the yard between Barrow's house and kitchen. When rebel men on foot and horseback reached his front yard, Barrow attempted to hold off the impending violence so his wife could escape out the back of their home and seek shelter in the swamps. When Mary Barrow exited her home, Lucy met her. She grabbed Mary Barrow and held her fast. She later was charged with conspiring to rebel, the only woman who was tried. Lucy would have been very familiar with the yard between the kitchen, the outbuildings, and the house. She knew to wait out back because she had used the entrances and exits daily in her labors as an enslaved woman. When she reached out and held fast to Mary Barrow's arm, she was stopping a woman who had supervised her labor, exerted power over her daily life, and in all likelihood visited physical violence upon her. Her access to the Barrow farm's spaces facilitated and defined her moment of participation in the Southampton Rebellion.[23]

The actions of Cynthia and Venus, other enslaved women in the neighborhood, exemplify how women maintained an intelligence network and supply line in yards and kitchens, sites of distinctly feminine work. Cynthia, who was enslaved by Jacob Williams, experienced the rebellion in the Williamses' farm kitchen, where she was at work with Williams's wife, Nancy. She was present when rebels entered the kitchen and murdered Nancy Williams and her young children. Then she began the cooking that needed to be done as their bodies lay on the kitchen floor.[24] Venus, who was at the Porter place where Richard Porter enslaved her, passed on information to a group of rebels as they moved through the county looking for sites for important meetings.[25] Each woman stayed on the farm where she labored each day and did not leave. Cynthia continued cooking, like Ester and Charlotte.[26] Venus took note of the comings and goings on the Porter place and passed on the vital information she had access to when others came looking for news.

In an instant, the spaces where white and Black women negotiated work and power every day became sites of resistance and survival, murder and attempted murder. Ester, Charlotte, Lucy, Cynthia, and Venus lived at similar sites of enslavement and worked at similar tasks. They were the rebels who remained to hold on to ground that the rebels had gained when their male counterparts moved on to the next farm. Ester, Charlotte, Lucy, and Cynthia faced their white female enslavers, took over their kitchens, and went about the work of sustaining the rebellion by preparing evening meals. Venus greeted rebels in the front yard, extending hospitality to Black men. The sites of women's daily labor—the yard, the kitchen, the front porch—were sites of confrontation and reckoning between white and Black women. The enslaved women had long done the daily work of resistance and survival. Claiming and holding distinctly feminine sites of labor transformed what were once spaces of oppression into spaces where each woman could live free for as long as the rebellion was alive.

The behavior of each woman during the rebellion is as important to consider as her behavior afterward. Ester and Charlotte each met with different ends. In 1900, William Sidney Drewry wrote in *The Southampton Insurrection* that Ester and Charlotte made their way to Cross Keys, where many white women and children sought refuge and the local militia held suspected rebels as prisoners. According to Drewry's interviews, Nathaniel Francis found Ester and embraced her for her loyalty. But Charlotte met a more gruesome fate; Nathaniel Francis "dragged her out, tied her to an oak tree, and she was riddled with bullets, he firing the first shot." Drewry reported that "the tree died from the number of shot[s] which pierced it."[27] There is no other documentation of Charlotte's death, and Ester's fate remains unknown.

Enslaved women and free women of color were embedded in networks of evasion and resistance. They navigated layered geographies of surveillance and control. They built geographies of evasion and resistance. These women demonstrate how those geographies become visible in Southampton County through women's actions. Women's knowledge of diverse sites of labor, their white enslavers, and communications networks contributed to the strategy of the male participants in the rebellion. Their gender-specific knowledge also influenced their own choices, as demonstrated by the divergent actions of Ester and Charlotte. Instead of labeling enslaved women as either for or against the rebellion, it is more useful to understand enslaved women as embedded in its path and its planning.

Every enslaved man present at the Cabin Pond meeting of rebels had important connections to enslaved women. Soon after the militia quelled

rebellion violence, enslaved women appeared at the county seat of Jerusalem for examination by attorneys in preparation for the trials of people they
knew or, in the case of Lucy, her own trial. Venus, Cynthia, and Lucy figured
in court proceedings after the rebellion, Venus and Cynthia as witnesses
and Lucy on trial for her life. While the records available mostly remember
them as witnesses or defendants, we know that their lived experiences
meant that they did not simply watch the rebellion as it happened. They
were agents of resistance and survival in their communities.

3

Free Issues

Free People of Color in Antebellum Southampton County

I was never a slave. My people was what
you call free issues. I was free born. . . .
De paddyrollers use to bother my father
somepin' awful. Dey'd come an' beat him
anytime.

—Mrs. Mollie Booker, born 1850, quoted in
Weevils in the Wheat

The cotton was nearing maturity in Southampton County by September
1831. Harvest was on the horizon, but an end to the trials and executions
that had begun in August was not. Eliza Crathenton, a free woman of color,
may have volunteered what she knew of Hardy, the man who was charged
with "consulting, advising, and conspiring to make insurrection & murder."[1]
She might have wondered whether the words of a free Black woman could
do anything to help him or she may have been coerced by white people's
threats to her own life. On September 7, 1831, seventeen days after the
chaos of rebellion erupted in Southampton County, Crathenton spoke in
Hardy's defense. The court clerk recorded her testimony as one sentence
in the Southampton County minute book: "The prisoner and two others
told her they meant to join Genl. Nat. and she dissuaded them from it."[2]
Although Eliza Crathenton was the only free woman of color to testify in
local trials after the rebellion, she was one of many free women and free

people of color who lived in Southampton County and endured the aftermath of the rebellion with enslaved people.

Free African Americans lived and labored all over the commonwealth.
Throughout Virginia's history, whites were simultaneously uneasy about the
presence of free people of color and reliant on the labor they supplied.[3] Historian Suzanne Lebsock best described the relationship of white Virginians
with free people of color: "In practice, periods of relatively benign neglect
alternated with spells of close surveillance and sudden repression. In law,
the story was one of progressive deterioration."[4] Free Black people were
always vulnerable, and they were particularly good scapegoats to whites
who were anxious to preserve their claims to mastery.

After the Southampton Rebellion, free people of color endured renewed
suspicion, violence, and hostility throughout the South.[5] White residents
of Southampton turned their animosity and suspicion toward free Black
people in the weeks after the rebellion, scrutinizing their role in the county's
labor economy and their ties to enslaved people. All over the commonwealth, white officials and legislators considered drastic economic and social
change. Legislators even debated the possibility of manumitting Virginia's
enslaved people. Ultimately, white leaders decided that free people of color
were the real problem in their slave society.[6]

In Southampton County and all over Virginia, free people of color bore
the brunt of reactionary legal changes after the rebellion. Slavery remained
the same and enslaved people remained human property. Free people of
color such as Eliza Crathenton faced a far more uncertain future. The local
interrogation of a handful of free Black men and the testimony of one free
woman demonstrate that whites considered free people of color to be potential agitators. At the state level, legislators argued for repressive actions
toward free Black people in the commonwealth that included expulsion.[7]

Free people of color built and contributed to the geographies of evasion
and resistance that both they and enslaved people relied on for survival.
Free status did not preclude living with and sharing in the struggles of
the enslaved. Free status did not mean an escape from violence and hu-
miliation at the hands of whites, and free Black people navigated the same
geographies of surveillance and control as their enslaved neighbors and
family members. In Virginia, the material condition of free people of color
often mirrored that of enslaved people, especially in the rural areas that
constituted most of the commonwealth. Freedom for African Americans

often meant living among enslaved people and doing similar work. In early nineteenth-century Southampton County, free Black people were a larger proportion of the population than in most Virginia counties and free people of color had access to many Black community spaces and geographies. They were arbiters of information, suppliers of support, and, at times, willing participants in the rebellion.

Demography of Freedom:
The Free Black People of Southampton

From 1790 to 1860, Southampton County was home to a population of free Black people that ranked in the top six largest populations of free people of color in the commonwealth. In 1800, the year Nat Turner was born, Southampton had the third largest free Black population in the state. Accomack County, home to the oldest free enclave in the commonwealth, had the largest population of free people of color. Nansemond County, Southampton's neighbor to the east, had the second largest. From 1800 to 1830, Southampton's population of free people remained one of the largest in the state. Free people of color there lived in one of three basic arrangements: on white-owned land, on Black-owned land, and on Indian Land reserved for the Cheroenhaka (Nottoway). Most free people of color worked for whites and lived on white-owned land. Archie Booker remembered a free Black enclave near his enslaver's land: "Some . . . wuz set free, some tu'ned free, an' some wuz free bo'n. My ol boss ustuh hire some o' em to wuk at harves time."[8] Physical proximity, shared labor regimes, and white violence and surveillance embedded free people of color in enslaved communities. Free people of color in antebellum Southampton County occupied a social category that was dynamic and vulnerable to white incursion and legal maneuvering.

Elite and middling white Virginians relied on the labor of free people of color to supplement their own labor force. For rural Virginians, especially owners of small to midsized farms, hiring a free person to do fieldwork that poor whites turned down as "negro work" was far cheaper than purchasing an enslaved person of prime working age. If a farmer could abide his or her enslaved people living with and intermingling with free people of color, hiring free Black people for the season was an affordable option. Some whites rented enslaved people from neighbors, but when they did so, they were required to pay the enslavers of the workers they hired at the end of the season. Free Black people did not command this kind of control over their wages. By the antebellum period, Virginia law had long dictated that free people of color could not provide evidence against whites. This made it difficult for them to challenge employers in cases of wage theft.[9]

White Virginians were committed to protecting their access to free Black laborers. They restricted the economic opportunities open to free Black people and limited their class mobility.[10] "White prejudice," writes Ira Berlin, "not natural law, barred free Negroes from full participation in Southern society. Whites in the Upper South frankly admitted this."[11] Although the terms for them changed from generation to generation, free Negroes, free Blacks, free people of color were always troublesome to whites. Free people of color may have done labor alongside enslaved people that whites would not, but they were very clear about the fact that they were not enslaved. Tom Hester remembered, "Us was different from de slaves, cause us was 'free-born' an' got to be paid fo' workin'."[12] In the wake of the Southampton Rebellion, white Virginians simultaneously defended local free people of color they had personal relationships with and supported legislation that would expel them from the Commonwealth of Virginia.[13]

Local census records are one indication of the economic importance of free Black laborers. Of the three major demographic groups in Southampton County—whites, free Black people, and enslaved people—the free Black population went through the most change in the period 1800 to 1830. Their population jumped in these decades from about 5.9 percent of the total population to nearly 10.85 percent, an increase from 829 people to 1,745 people. This swell in population was the result of factors that were common in the Upper South: natural increase, a rash of manumissions in the early national period, and even some migration from other areas.

Free people of color remained in Southampton County because they found work there. They also remained because Virginia's vagrancy laws limited their mobility in the commonwealth. Antebellum Virginia law required free African Americans to register with county officials each year, for which they paid a fee.[14] Whites used these registries as tools of surveillance and to control free Black mobility. In 1793, legislators prohibited free people of color by law from living or traveling outside the counties where they were registered as free persons. In subsequent revisions of the code in the early nineteenth century, lawmakers further restricted the mobility of free people by introducing new fines and punishments for leaving the place where they had registered. Those who traveled outside the counties where they were registered risked imprisonment, fines, and possible indentured servitude to pay the fine if they were caught. Employers who hired a free Black person who was not registered in their home county risked a $5 fine. White officials and residents surveilled free Black people by recording important identifying information, including place of residence and physical appearance, in registries of free Black people.[15]

In St. Luke's Parish, owners of smaller farms who had cash crops to get in needed supplementary labor throughout the agricultural cycle. Their use of cheap free laborers of color made it possible for them to farm such crops. The extant free negro registries that officials used to track the residences and occupations of free Black people reveal that free people of color lived all over the county in the decade leading to the rebellion. Local officials organized registries based on county parishes. Free people of color lived in both Nottoway and St. Luke's Parishes. Very few people of color lived on their own land, on land owned by other free African Americans, in free Black households on land designated as poor land or on the local Cheroenhaka (Nottoway) Indian reservation.[16] In each half of the county, free people of color had limited choices in terms of both housing and the work whites made available in the geographic areas they were confined to.

Very few free Black people owned their own farms.[17] Only a small number of free people of color lived and worked without white supervision and surveillance. In 1821, a decade before the Southampton Rebellion, 12 percent of free people of color in St. Luke's Parish lived on Black-owned land. In contrast, 71 percent of the free African American population lived on white-owned land and 3 percent were listed as transient. The remaining 14 percent of the registered free people of color in St. Luke's lived on Indian Land. At that time, Virginia law recognized both free people of African descent and Indigenous people as free people of color.[18] The two communities overlapped at times and were sometimes intimately connected through kinship networks and marriage to each other and to enslaved people. Local officials surveilled Indian Land and its residents just as they ordered patrols of enslaved people's dwellings and curtailed free Black people's mobility.

For most, there was no affordable alternative to living on white-owned land. Some free people of color lived and worked on white farms to be near their enslaved family members. The local overseers of the poor bound out others as children to local adults, often whites, to pay off their parents' debts or to house them because they were orphans. Skilled laborers sought employment on white farms because that was where they could get work. However, extant registries make clear that the vast majority of free men of color worked as agricultural laborers in Southampton county. Laboring for white landowners was often the only employment available to free Black men, particularly in rural areas. Earning enough to purchase their own land was difficult and out of reach for many free men of color.[19]

Officials recorded free people of color as members of white households and not as their own autonomous households in census records. Free negro registries most often list white households as the place of residence for free people. Free people of color frequently worked with enslaved people at the same tasks, in the same fields and outbuildings. The most popular form of hired free Black labor required white employers to provide room and board that was often similar in quality to that provided for enslaved labor.[20]

Whites of all classes recognized the economic advantages of hiring free people of color. John Urquhart, one of Southampton's most prominent residents, enslaved over 100 people. In 1822, he employed ten free people of color.[21] He hired four free Black men to clear swampland and dig irrigation ditches. Urquhart, a wealthy landowner with a large enslaved workforce, used cheap, expendable labor to dig the ditches his property needed.[22] This was dangerous work that exposed the men to injury and disease. Urquhart thus protected his investment in enslaved labor by exploiting free men of color. Jim Urquhart, a free Black shoemaker, and his wife, also a free person of color, lived on John Urquhart's property. The remaining four free people of color listed, two male farmers and two spinsters, were named Green. One of the ditchers also had the surname Green, and it is possible that they were all related. Whether Urquhart employed them for years or for seasonal work, their presence in his household demonstrates how whites of all classes relied on free Black laborers.

Most of Southampton's white residents were nowhere near as wealthy as Urquhart. Most who hired free people of color used them in the fields as supplemental agricultural labor. On many farms along the path of the rebellion, free Black people worked alongside men and women who would later participate in the violence of the rebellion.[23] During the rebellion, the Jacob Williams farm was directly in the path of the rebels. There, they murdered Williams's wife and three of their children; the wife of Williams's overseer, Mrs. Caswell Worrell, and her two children; and Edwin Drewry, a business associate of Jacob Williams.[24] After the Southampton Rebellion, Nelson, who was enslaved by Williams, would stand trial for his involvement in the uprising.

Household composition is important for assessing how and why whites decided to employ free people of color. Jacob Williams's farm and labor force illustrate a common way whites used an integrated free and enslaved labor force. Before the rebellion, Jacob Williams enslaved six Black adults. Only four of his enslaved laborers were potentially in their prime; one was too old and one was too young to be counted among his prime labor force. The seven free adult people of color who lived on his place accounted for over half of his hands.[25] All but one of the free people listed in census records for Jacob Williams's household were women. Most of the Black people residing on the Williams farm were free and female.[26]

The Williams case was not an anomaly. Census records document a visible and valuable population of free women whom whites employed as free laborers all along the rebellion path. For example, Edwin Barns enslaved only two elderly people in 1830 and drew labor from the eleven free people of color who resided on his farm. Only four were free adults and three of those were free women of color.[27] Black women, even free women, were eligible for fieldwork along with any number of domestic tasks. Free women of color were versatile like their enslaved counterparts; they could be relied on to tend crops, supplement domestic labor, and help process agricultural produce throughout Southampton County.

The households of Richard Porter, Nathaniel Francis, and James W. Parker illustrate the most common labor configuration in the county. Their enslaved property outnumbered the free Black people they employed. Free people of color were supplementary labor in these households. All three employed nearly equal numbers of free Black men and free Black women. Richard Porter, who enslaved thirty people in 1830, was not a member of Southampton's tiny number of gentlemen, but he was doing quite well for himself and his family, as were Francis and Parker. Of those enslaved on Porter's farm, nineteen were either half or partial hands, given their ages. This meant that only 30 percent of his enslaved property, eleven adult full hands, were at his disposal to tend and bring in each year's crop. Fieldwork was not the only work that would have needed tending to on the Porter place. His white family included eight children and only two adult women. It is no surprise that Porter employed a free woman of color and that his household included a young free boy.[28] Both would have been helpful on a farm where Porter needed the women he enslaved in the fields during the agricultural cycle.

Elsewhere in the neighborhood, Nathaniel Francis's labor force looked slightly different. His household included Charlotte and Ester, two enslaved women, but the majority of his enslaved workforce was male. Among his free laborers was one free woman of color, again perhaps to offset the times in the agricultural cycle when enslaved women were needed to do agricultural work or because she was kin to one of the enslaved people on his farm.[29] The adult prime workforce of another neighbor, James W. Parker, included only one free person of color, a man of prime working age, among ten Black adults. Free men, women, and children lived in small numbers all over the rebellion route; they were a visible and vital part of the Black community. While free Black people were 10.85 percent of the total population, they were almost 20 percent of the Black population by 1830.[30] Households such as those of Parker, Francis, Porter, and Williams, all of which featured significantly in the Southampton Rebellion, demonstrate how embedded the free 20 percent of the Black community was among people who were enslaved.

A small group of free African Americans lived on Black-owned farms in the 1820s and 1830s. They also lived in close proximity to whites and enslaved people. In the 1820s, roughly 12 percent of the free Black people listed in St. Luke's Parish lived on Black-owned land. This small group consisted of only fourteen households. Of those fourteen, only three resided on their own land. The members of the other eleven households lived on land owned by other free Black people.

Jonas Cosby, a resident of St. Luke's Parish who lived with his wife and their four children, is a typical example of this small group of Black landowners. Cosby had done well for himself after his enslaver manumitted him in his will in the early 1800s.[31] In 1804, he married Pricilla Hunt, with whom he had four children over the next sixteen years. In 1820, Cosby's household included ten members, all free people of color.[32] This included Cosby's immediate family of six and four free adult people of color. By 1822, his household included fifteen; five more children had been added. James Hunt, who was possibly related to Cosby's wife, is the only other adult man listed. Pricilla, whom officials listed as Mrs. Jonas Cosby, was one of four adult women. The other three were Lotty Byrd; Tamar Byrd, who had one child; and Evey Artis, a single woman with four children. Children who were younger than working age accounted for more than half of the population on the Cosby place, as was the case in the other free households of color in St. Luke's Parish. In the Cosby household, free people of color may have formed a small enclave, but their neighbors were white landowners. Slavery and enslavers surrounded them.

Southampton was also home to the area's first people, by the 1830s a small but visible Indigenous population. In 1831,the Cheroenhaka (Nottoway) still had a reservation in St. Luke's Parish that was sometimes called "the old circle and square" because of the shape of its boundaries. However, it was officially noted as Indian Land. The people listed in extant Southampton County free negro registries who lived on Indian Land could have been Native Americans, mixed-raced people, or free Black people with kinship ties to Indigenous people. Historian Arica Coleman notes that "identification of American Indians or part American Indian people as Indian by census takers and county authorities prior to the Civil War was the exception, not the rule."[33] This was certainly the case in antebellum Virginia. White Virginians referred to Virginia's Indigenous people as mulattoes, negroes, and colored. State and local laws in the commonwealth often included Indigenous people under the umbrella category of "all other free persons," and some free negro registries include Indigenous people and groups. In Southampton County, officials included free people of color who lived on Indian Land on free negro registries. The Cheroenhaka (Nottoway) had a long history of community and kinship ties with both enslaved and free Black people in the county. Oral tradition among contemporary Cheroenhaka people says that Indian Land in the county was a refuge for Black people during waves of white violence, including after the Southampton Rebellion.[34]

Existing records of free households on Indian Land reveal the prevalence of mixed-raced and mixed-status households on the Cheroenhaka (Nottoway) reservation.[35] The free negro registry for St. Luke's Parish for 1822 lists twenty-three family groups on Indian Land.[36] Only three couples were identified as parents to the (unnamed) children on the list. Single adults, sometimes listed with children, account for the remaining nineteen households. Five women whom officials recorded as unmarried lived with their children on Indian land.[37] Four men with no listed spouse were recorded with at least one child. In antebellum Virginia, any number of reasons could account for this. The death of one parent, status as free or enslaved, or the adoption of orphaned kin could result in families with one adult. While some of those listed could have been Cheroenhaka or of partial Cheroenhaka descent, the register demonstrates that the legal status of Virginia's Indigenous peoples and free Black people overlapped in ways that influenced connected social networks.

Free people of color of all racial backgrounds had to navigate the geography of surveillance and control that white Virginians carefully constructed to practice mastery over enslaved people. Proximity to whites and enslaved people was key to defining the experiences of free people of color. Free people of color mostly lived close to whites as members of their hybrid enslaved and free labor forces. White neighbors surrounded those who lived on Indian Land or Black-owned land, as did enslaved Black neighbors.

However, yearly registration, fines, and close proximity do not fully describe the geography of surveillance and control free people of color navigated. Free people were vulnerable to white violence. Their freedom was tenuous and their status as residents of Southampton was in heightened jeopardy after the rebellion. White whims, anxieties, and power carefully circumscribed a set of legal rights that restricted and hindered their freedom with each passing generation. To endure, free people of color built and maintained meaningful solidarities with enslaved people that contributed to the county's geography of evasion and resistance.

Free Women's Access to Geographies of Evasion and Resistance

Free women of color occupied a specific labor niche that gave them the greatest access to Southampton's many layered geographies of evasion and resistance. Their work placed them in close proximity to both the white and Black communities of Southampton. Their mobility on and off farms made them key sources of information and counsel. Unlike enslaved women, free Black women had the potential for mobility off the farms and plantations where they found work. This made them important assets to the geography of evasion and resistance that enslaved people and free people of color maintained in the county.

Gender played a role in defining the kinds of labor free Black people did. Men were primarily agricultural laborers. All but the poorest white women in the period were able to escape field labor and do domestic labor for their households. The wealthiest managed full staffs of enslaved domestics. The middling white women of Southampton county used a combination of free and enslaved women to support them as they took on the domestic labor for their households. Free women of color rarely worked solely for their kin. As Mrs. Octavia Featherstone remembered, "No, none of us was ever slaves. A white woman asked me several weeks ago had I been a slave. I tol' her, 'No.'" Featherstone continued, "Den she asked how did we all get long makin' a livin'. I got fretted an' said, 'No, I've never been hungry in my life. Yes, I was a free Negro.' My mother an' gramma work for us five children."[38] Featherstone's mother and grandmother, like many other free Black women in Virginia, worked to provide for their families.

A very small number of men practiced trades or did nonagricultural manual labor in the county. In St. Luke's Parish, David Byrd and Patrick Artis worked as tailors and Stephen Barham made shoes.[39] Nottoway Parish was home to ten free Black shoemakers, a hatter, and two carpenters in the decade before the Southampton Rebellion. By the middle of the 1820s, Nottoway Parish also had two free Black coopers. In both parishes, a small number of free Black men were sawyers, ditchers, and waggoneers. In addition, Stephen Barsham, who lived in Nottoway Parish, earned money as a fiddler in 1826.[40] This small number of free men was far outnumbered by their free counterparts who earned a livelihood as farmers or agricultural laborers.[41]

Working as a tradesman or laborer in antebellum Southampton County did not guarantee mobility or freedom from white surveillance during the workday. Of the free men of color who registered with the county, only two who owned their own land were tradesmen and only four had mobility built into their workday. Waggoneers Anthony Newsome and Phil Thompson traveled during working hours making deliveries. Carpenters Jim Cotton and Jem Colt, who owned their own land, may have had to travel to complete jobs or deliver their work. Most of the tradesmen and laborers among Southampton's free Black community were forced to rely on whites for access to housing. In St. Luke's Parish, only one free Black tradesman lived on land that was owned by another person of color. Even for those who managed to own land, residency and registration requirements significantly curtailed their mobility.

Local officials almost always recorded some type of work next to the names of free women of color. In St. Luke's Parish in 1822, only ten women were listed without an occupation in the registry. All of them were married or kin to free Black men and were listed as members of their households.[42] Certainly these women worked. Domestic labor, supplementary farm labor, and parenting were physically demanding in the antebellum period. It is likely that these women did domestic labor. When parents or local overseers of the poor bound out free girls of color, instruction in housekeeping was always listed as the skill their new masters would train them in.[43] Domestic work, including work as a laundress, was one of the few forms of employment available to free women of color. Over the course of a free woman's life, she might perform domestic labor and hire herself out as needed to supplement family income. While officials may have left blank spaces for a handful of free women of color in extant records, that does not mean that those women did not do seasonal work.

Most free women of color registered as adults with occupations. In 1822, Jinny Briggs, who lived with her husband Jacob and their four children on land owned by James Brett in St. Luke's Parish, was listed as a farmer.[44] Only two other free women of color were listed as farmers in the registry that year, and both of them were connected to free Black men in Nottoway Parish. Mrs. Harry Brown lived with her husband and their five children on land John Scott owned, and Grace Holland, a free Black woman with a child and no listed spouse, lived in the household of Jason Gardner, a free Black landowner. It is possible that more women worked as farm laborers. Harvest time may have required women's hands in the fields or for processing work. But the fact that few free Black women were registered with the occupation of farmer denotes that women with that status may have avoided fieldwork when they could and that white male officials were willing to record them as something other than field laborers, in contrast to enslaved women.[45]

Free Black women in both Nottoway and St. Luke's Parishes almost always appear in records with the occupation of spinster. In this case, the term refers to the occupation of spinning rather than to marital status.[46] The term defined a specific kind of work or whites would not have included it and free women would not have identified it as their occupation. Both married women and those listed without spouses appear as spinsters. Women with and without children, women who lived on land owned by free Black people, women who lived on white-owned land, and women who lived on Indian Land all appear as spinsters in the county's free negro registries. The entry for Molly Mckill, who lived in St. Luke's Parish in 1822, listed her occupations as spinster and waiter. Even Sally Gardner, a free woman who owned her own land where seventeen other free people of color lived, was listed in the Nottoway Parish registry in 1826 as a spinster.

Spinning cotton into yarn and then weaving it into homespun cloth was prevalent in the 1820s and 1830s in Southampton County. Women may have traveled to spin in weaving cottages on farms throughout the county or to take in fiber to spin.[47] That would have given free women who were spinsters mobility that free men did not have. Free women of color who were spinsters may have had the greatest mobility within the Black community in Southampton County.

White and Black women did the majority of the work needed to produce clothing. This labor connected fields to weaving cottages to houses. Enslaved women processed cotton before and after ginning. If they could be spared from the fields, they joined white women and free Black women to produce clothing by spinning, weaving, dyeing, and sewing. Whites assigned free women of color, like enslaved women, flexible gendered labor. This afforded Black women the possibility of greater mobility within the bounds of farms and connected free and enslaved women in the context of their workday. This connection to enslaved people is the context in which whites judged the potential danger of allowing free people of color to remain in Southampton County and the commonwealth.

Free People of Color on Trial:
Learning from Eliza Crathenton

It is difficult to determine the full extent of the violence free and enslaved African Americans endured after the rebellion in Southampton County.[48] Often officials listed Black people simply as "suspected rebels" in the documents they produced about post-rebellion white violence, making it hard to determine who was free and who was not. For example, one militia company from outside Southampton decapitated at least fifteen suspected rebels and placed their heads on pikes at a crossroads long known as Black Head Signpost. While there is a record of this event, we do not know which unfortunate African Americans met this horrific end.[49] What is known is that an attorney took Eliza Crathenton's deposition in defense of an enslaved man on trial for involvement in the rebellion while severed heads rotted in the August heat.

Crathenton's one-line defense of Hardy, an enslaved man, provides clues to her position in the community. First, Hardy's attorney thought she had some credibility as a witness. The line between coercion and free choice remained thin in the days after the rebellion, especially for Black women. It is possible that she came forward as a matter of necessity because of the threat of violence. Available sources to do not reveal her relationship to Hardy. Was he kin? Would she have come forward on her own to defend him? According to Crathenton, Hardy and two others spoke with her about their plans to seek out the band of rebels who moved through the county. She testified that she told them not to join in the rebellion. She positioned herself as trustworthy and wise, someone men might seek advice from before risking their lives. It is not clear that the men sought her advice, but we know that they trusted her with knowledge of their intent to join the rebellion. Her testimony states that she "dissuaded them." She told them not to join and believed they had heeded her counsel. Hardy and his attorney hoped that local justices would believe her.[50]

Free people of color were both witnesses and suspected rebels in the trials that followed the rebellion. In all, the court examined five free people for possible involvement in the rebellion: Arnold Artes, Thomas Hathcock, Exum Artist, Isham Turner, and Berry Newsom.[51] Local magistrates had limited authority over free people suspected of capital offenses. Virginia law stated that only Virginia's state courts could try free people of color. However, county officials examined each man. All were later tried in the state's superior court.

It is not difficult to imagine how they ended up in the company of the enslaved rebels. They worked alongside enslaved people and were connected to the enslaved community economically and socially. They suffered under the same system of surveillance and control. For those same reasons it is not difficult to understand why Eliza Crathenton told Hardy, an enslaved man, not to run off and join an uprising that, victory or no victory, ensured white violence against Black people. If that was her motivation, she was not wrong. The days and months following the rebellion were plenty violent.

Whites harbored the perception that the mere presence of free people of color could inspire rebellion. They were not entirely wrong. Free men of color were present at major rebellion sites. Those suspected of involvement in the rebellion gave testimony in cases that involved enslaved people. Free men stood trial for their possible participation in the rebellion. Before remanding them to jail, justices interviewed Thomas Haithcock (sometimes Hathcock), Exum Artist (sometimes Artes), Isham Turner, Arnold Artes (sometimes Artist), and Berry Newsom, a free apprentice of color, before discharging them for further prosecution in the superior court.[52] The court also heard Thomas Haithcock as a witness in another enslaved man's trial. The involvement of free people of color in the Southampton Rebellion was not a figment of the imagination of anxious white people. But free people of color were part of the fabric of Black resistance in the county rather than its sole originators.

Eliza Crathenton's brief appearance in the trial record gives us one clue about how free women could have endured the rebellion: wary of the consequences, they offered advice, welcome or not, against joining the rebellion. In Hardy's case, local justices judged him guilty and sentenced him to death. They valued him at $450. And then, as they did with other defendants to whom they wanted to grant their version of mercy, they recommended that the governor of Virginia commute his sentence to sale from the commonwealth.[53] The fact that he had known about the rebellion and had not acted to defend or warn whites tainted him and made it impossible for justices charged with ensuring the safety of Southampton's whites to allow him to return to his life as an enslaved man on Benjamin Edwards's farm. It is possible that Crathenton's assurance that she had dissuaded Hardy held some sway with the court. Perhaps Hardy's defense attorney was right to lean on Eliza Crathenton's credibility and status in the Black community, status that even whites may have been aware of.

By October 1831, the month after Crathenton gave her testimony, white Virginians began a petition campaign to push for the gradual emancipation of the commonwealth's considerable enslaved population. In December, the General Assembly of Virginia began debating the issue of manumission. As debates came to a close in January 1832, six months after the rebellion and two months after Nat Turner's execution, Virginia's most prominent men decided that slavery should remain unchanged in the commonwealth. In the coming years, Virginia's legislators would recommit to the long-standing ban on the in-migration of free people of color to the commonwealth and Virginians would increase their support for colonization efforts like the one that sent some of Southampton's free Black people to West Africa just after the rebellion. In 1831, legislators passed an act that required free people of color who remained in the state in violation of the law to be sold at auction, and the state constitution of 1851 "reiterated that slaves emancipated after that date would 'forfeit their freedom by remaining in the Commonwealth more than twelve months.'"[54] However, whites enforced the statute that required newly manumitted people to leave Virginia within a year of their emancipation unevenly.[55]

In the immediate aftermath of the rebellion, white violence against free Black people spread far and wide. As famed fugitive from slavery Harriet Jacobs remembered, "The news threw our town into great commotion." Jacobs remembered how whites terrorized free Black people in her coastal North Carolina hometown of Edenton. She concluded wryly, "Strange that they should be alarmed when their slaves were so 'contented and happy'! But so it was."[56]

White suspicion against free people of color may have amounted to nothing in some corners of the commonwealth, but in Southampton County, some free Black people were on the move after the rebellion in response to white violence. In late October 1831, 245 free Black people set sail for Liberia, joining a wave of migration to West Africa that one of the county's prominent whites funded. By the end of 1832, an additional sixty-six free Black people had left Southampton for the shores of West Africa.[57] In official documents, others disappeared from households where they had once appeared. For example, in 1830, six free people of color lived on the farm of Nathaniel Francis, who lost almost his entire white family to the rebellion. Ten years later, the only African Americans on the Francis place were enslaved.[58] Some landowners may have chosen to hire enslaved people from other enslavers or buy more of their own instead of hiring free Black people.

Free people of color were vital to the county's labor economy and to its African American community. Their labor and their living arrangements often integrated them with enslaved laborers. These arrangements also brought them under the same surveillance as enslaved people. All but a very few free men of color lived and worked on the county's small to mid-sized farms. For free women, even seasonal work spinning local cotton and processing fibers into cloth and clothing provided mobility on farms throughout the workday. The pace of mixed agriculture dictated their lives just as much as it dictated the lives for enslaved people and whites.

Free people of color, and free women like Eliza Crathenton in particular, had access to various community spaces and geographies. They were sources of information, suppliers of support, and, at times, willing participants in the rebellion. The white power structure did not overlook this role in their community. Ultimately, whites in Virginia did very little to change the institution of slavery in the wake of the rebellion, but they continued to chip away at and deny freedoms to free people of color in the commonwealth.

Free people played a distinct role in Black strategies for survival before, during, and after the rebellion in ways that are hidden to the archival records and in ways that such records expose. Eliza Crathenton's counsel during the rebellion and her deposition and community standing after the rebellion may well have saved Hardy's life. When her brief appearance in the court record is considered in the context of Black Southampton's resistive networks, it demonstrates how Black people parsed their words in a way that helped their own chances for survival. In her short appearance in surviving records, Crathenton was also a member of the network that ensured Hardy's survival. Women like her were embedded in labor forces on farms and in Black communities all over the neighborhood.

4

Generation, Resistance, and Survival

African American Children and the Southampton Rebellion

Lord, I done been thew somepin'. When I'se
five years ole I had to wuk. . . . A few years
after dat I was put out in de fiel's to wuk all
day. Sometimes I wished I could run away.

—Miss Caroline Hunter, born 1847 near
   Suffolk, Virginia, quoted in *Weevils in the
   Wheat*

Young Moses remembered turning in for the night on August 21, 1831. He slept in the kitchen, a coveted resting space for enslaved people during the winter months. Uninsulated cellars or cabins were unbearable when snow and freezing rain blanketed Virginia. For Moses, the kitchen provided warmth from long-burning fires needed to prepare food or wash clothes.

There were plenty of reasons why a white enslaver would allow a boy of his age to sleep in the farm's kitchen each night: he could look after the fire, he could haul in more fuel, he could fetch water at first light, and when early morning cooking began, he could set out to tend the farm's livestock. Perhaps on a farm the size of Joseph Travis's, one with only seventeen enslaved people, the kitchen housed more than just Moses. While some farms and plantations in the neighborhood had quarters in rows behind the house where white enslavers lived, many more landowners housed their human property in a more haphazard manner. On some farms, whites bunked with enslaved people in the same structure; on others, enslaved people lived in outbuildings; and on some farms, there was a bit of both.[1]

Although the kitchen was detached from the main dwelling, it was a social hub. While many a landowner imagined that their house was the center of their small kingdom, the kitchen more often was the farm's nerve center. Everyone, white and Black, had some interaction with the farm's kitchen. News came through the kitchen and moved out to the fields or up to the house. The produce of the farm moved from field to hands to kitchen to hands to pot to hands to mouth. The kitchen was the center where white and Black women labored to keep the entire household alive.[2]

The Travises' kitchen also received visitors. As Moses lay his head down on the warm evening in August, an enslaved man named Jack was visiting from Jordan Barnes's farm. Jack was owned by William Reece, who had hired him out to Barnes. It is likely that Jack was a frequent visitor to the Travis place; it is possible that Jack's sister lived there with her husband Hark. So it was probably not out of the ordinary for Jack to be visiting in the kitchen. Moses later remembered that Jack was there as he drifted off to sleep.[3]

Moses was awakened earlier than usual on the morning of August 22 by the sound of commotion in the yard. Jack was sitting with his head in his hands, obviously sick. He was weeping. And Moses heard more noise and activity from the barn. From the yard, he and Jack could hear commands. Nat Turner, a man from his farm, was drilling a group of enslaved men in organized ranks. Among the men who stood and marched on Turner's command were well-known enslaved men from the neighborhood. Moses would have recognized Hark, a man he knew well. He would have also known Will, a man who lived on the Francis farm, who was moving among the men holding a bloody axe. What an odd sight to have seen in the very early hours of the morning: Black men in ranks just like the local militia. Taking it all in, Moses may or may not have understood what the men were doing so early in the morning. But Jack's tears made an impression. Something was wrong. When the men exited the barn, Moses watched as Hark bullied Jack into moving forward with the assembled group. It was then that Moses most likely realized what had happened: the men of his neighborhood were in rebellion and his enslaver and his enslaver's family were dead.[4] He had

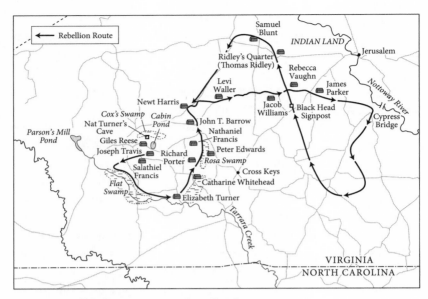

Map 3. The Rebellion Route. Map by Bill Nelson.

woken up in the middle of a slave rebellion. Most frightening of all, these men were insistent that he ride along with them.[5]

The Travis place where Moses lived was the first farm the rebels attacked on August 22, 1831 (see map 3). They entered the home of Joseph Travis and murdered every white man, woman, and child present. While Moses slept in the kitchen, a group of six enslaved men ate a stolen pig, drank their enslavers' brandy, and decided at a nearby pond that the time was finally right to launch what would become America's most famous slave rebellion.[6] Moses knew at least three of the men well: Nat Turner, Hark, and Jack all had connections to or lived on the Travis farm with him. He'd worked alongside them and seen them about the Travis place. That morning, he would travel with them as they tore through his neighborhood.[7]

Enslaved children and youths such as Moses witnessed, participated in, and testified about the Southampton Rebellion. The event involved not one but several generations of enslaved and free African Americans. While the best-known participants were grown men, children and youths played an important role both during the rebellion and in its immediate aftermath. The Black men who rose in violent rebellion thought it was important to take at least four enslaved boys in their early teens along with them. The prominent white men charged with keeping order in Southampton County ordered militia members to capture suspected rebels instead of killing them on sight. Among those taken and held in jail were four enslaved boys ages thirteen to fifteen and one young free Black apprentice. White officials tried the enslaved boys and interrogated the apprentice.[8] The actions and testimonies of this handful of boys and youths were important to both the white and Black men of Southampton County, a reminder to historians that the lives and labor of children are of equal importance to those of adults in the study of enslaved people's resistance.[9]

Children's experiences of the Southampton Rebellion demonstrate that they were valuable community members and that the adults who plotted the rebellion did so while thinking past their own lifetimes. Nat Turner and the enslaved men who planned and executed the Southampton Rebellion lived on farms that were home to other men, women, and children, Black and white, free and enslaved. While some may have had very self-interested motivations for participating in the Southampton Rebellion, all acted in the context of intersecting communities of enslaved people, free people of color, and whites across farms in Southampton County. Children were demographically significant in most antebellum communities. Whites took special care to account for both enslaved and free Black children because of their value as laborers and property and because of their connection to potential financial success. African Americans valued, trained, and nurtured Black children. At times, minding and training Black (and white) was part of the labor coerced from Black adults.[10]

Moses, who was described as a boy in his many appearances in South-ampton's county court records, was one of the many children who lived in Nat Turner's neighborhood. This chapter explores his life and that of the other enslaved children authorities prosecuted for involvement in the re-bellion. Using the testimonies of the formerly enslaved and the court cases related to specific Southampton County children, it is possible to trace the generational transfer of resistive practices and resistive attitudes, beliefs, and survival strategies. The careful training that enslaved adults took it upon themselves to provide Black children helped them survive and resist enslavement effectively.[11] Family and kinship were integral to African American resistive and survival practices and children were necessarily a part of these strategies.[12] The archival documents related to the Southampton Rebellion more readily yield the story of enslaved men, but with careful attention, those sources also provide information about the experiences of children during that turbulent time. Black children appear throughout these court records as participants in, witnesses to, and survivors of the Southampton Rebellion. Their appearance in court records as defendants and witnesses suggest ways that children were involved in adult resistive action, how resistive practices were passed from generation to generation, and how children's places in the community could have served a unique function amid the chaos and violence of the rebellion.[13]

The enslaved youths named Nathan, Tom, Davy, and Moses all were tried for their suspected participation in the rebellion. Officials called Daniel, Beck, and Moses to testify about the actions of adults and other children and youths during the rebellion. At least one free youth of color, Berry Newsom, was executed for his enthusiastic support of the rebellion. Although historians have overlooked these children and youths, they were in the middle of the court proceedings. From August through November of 1831, these children were far from forgotten.[14]

Childhood, Labor, and Survival in Southampton County

When they arrived in Southampton's jail in late August 1831, Moses, Nathan, Tom, Davy, and Berry Newsom were all young laborers who had great potential to appreciate in value as they grew into adulthood. They were among the nearly fifty prisoners held for trial as local white authorities attempted to assert control over Southampton's white and Black residents while they searched for answers about the rebellion's leaders. The authorities desperately wanted to reestablish themselves as county leaders who had law and order in the county firmly in hand. They knew that local enslavers expected them to protect the valuable adult male full hands, a substantial amount of enslaved property, that they held in the local jail. To keep law and custom, local white elites needed to value enslaved prisoners in court proceedings and see that their enslavers were compensated if local courts decided to condemn defendants to death or sell them away from Virginia.[15] Moses, at least, aided them considerably in their decision making.

The roles that Black children and youths, free and enslaved, played in Southampton's labor economy and social structure provides one set of clues about why local justices bothered to consider each youth's participation in the rebellion. All four were in their early teens in 1831 and were not yet full hands that could work at an adult capacity. But even at a reduced capacity for labor, they would have been of value on their farms. The harvest season had arrived and every hand was required, regardless of age.

Children were everywhere in Southampton County in the early antebellum period. In 1830, enslaved people below the age of 10 constituted 36 percent of the total enslaved population of the county. Free children of color under the age of 10 constituted nearly 43 percent of the total free Black population in the county. The neighborhood around Cross Keys, where most of the rebellion's violent activity happened and that provided a majority of its adult participants, consisted of small to midsized farms. Almost all of them housed enslaved and free children.[16]

Joseph Travis, the man who owned the farm where Moses lived, headed a household of twenty-two people. When he married the widow Sally Moore in October 1829 and brought her to live on his farm, she brought her young son Putnam with her. Just before the rebellion broke out, Travis and Sally welcomed the arrival of their first child, who was so young that their name and sex were not recorded in any documents.[17] The remaining seventeen members of the household were enslaved people. As part of his inheritance from his deceased father, Putnam Moore enslaved some of those seventeen people, including Nat Turner. Joseph Travis enslaved others. The total number of enslaved residents on the Travis place can be deceiving. Six of the seventeen enslaved members of the Travis household were children under the age of 10. The other enslaved boys who were involved in the Southampton Rebellion lived on a similar farm.

Nathaniel Francis, who enslaved Charlotte and Ester, was Joseph Travis's brother-in-law. He was a farmer with a number of community connections. Like the Travis farm, the Francis place was home both to white victims of the rebellion and rebellious enslaved people. Nathan, Tom, and Davy were among the human property the Francises kept. All three were captured and arrested after the rebellion. Three free children of color, six enslaved children, and two other Black youths lived on the Francis place.[18]

On some farms in the neighborhood, African American children constituted a similar or even greater proportion of the enslaved population. For example, Catharine Whitehead, another rebellion victim, enslaved 27 people in 1830; 11 of them, or 40 percent, were under the age of 9. Additionally,

Whitehead had one white child in her care. The children on the neighborhood's farms were not isolated from the adults. In those numbers, they
would have been underfoot.[19]

Free and enslaved African American children played distinctive roles in
both the slave economy and in their communities.[20] Many of them labored
in the fields.[21] While infants and toddlers often escaped field labor, some
enslavers used very young children to do simple tasks. They counted on
children to grow into valuable adult laborers and integrated children into
labor regimes early. Enslaved adults could both mind and train enslaved
children at the same time.

The gang labor system, which was favored in Virginia, divided enslaved
people into gangs based on their ability. While gang one would have been
made up of only the strongest adult hands, gangs two and three would
have had a place for older youths and children. Young boys and girls could
easily be employed in the third, or "trash," gang that followed the faster
and stronger first and second gangs as they tended and harvested upland
short-staple cotton. Given the small size of the farms and holdings of most
of Southampton's enslavers, children could have constituted the entire
"trash" gang during the fall harvest on many farms.[22]

There would have been any number of jobs for young hands outside
the fields. While enslaved children could not lift as much or pick as fast,
they often did auxiliary tasks as they learned adult laboring skills. As they
worked in slower gangs in the fields, wound yarn into balls in the weaving
cottage, fetched tools, and hauled water, for example, they observed adult
laborers and learned the skills needed to labor as an adult. During times
of the heaviest demand for labor, enslaved children were often required to
take on adult tasks, even if at a slower pace. Someone had to chop wood,
help in the dairy, run errands to neighboring farms, and help in the fields
by chasing off vermin and assisting in the annual harvest. While very young
children may have been exempt from daily labor, it is hard to imagine that
those who could walk, speak, and learn simple tasks would have remained
idle until they could enter the adult work world.[23]

Many white households included free children of color. Some were the
offspring of free adults who lived in white households. But as antebellum
county records attest, a number of free children were bound to white masters and mistresses.[24] The system of apprenticing orphans and children
whose parents could not provide for them, long the method of providing

for poor and orphaned children in England, was written into the legal code of colonial Virginia.[25] Indenture contracts bound children and the right to their labor to a specific adult master, in effect making it unlikely that a child would leave as long as their master remained in the county. Boys remained in service until they turned 21, while girls' terms finished when they were 18. Parents and the local ministers of the poor bound out children and even infants to those who promised to provide room, board, and some form of practical training.

Moses, Nathan, Tom, and Davy, who were 15 and younger, were not infants or toddlers. They were well on their way to becoming half-hands by the summer of 1831. The four young people grew up on similar small plantations where their labor would have been essential. Neither Nathaniel Francis nor Joseph Travis were among the gentry of Southampton County. One historian described the Francises as "prosperous but certainly not elite."[26] Nathaniel Francis owned fifteen enslaved laborers and employed three free Black adults. He supported his mother and his orphaned nephews.[27] In the fall of 1830, he took a wife and started his family with promising prospects. Neither very poor nor very rich, Nathaniel Francis and his family belonged to the closest thing the American South had to a middle class. This meant that although he was comfortable, he needed all available hands to ensure his farm's success. His mother, his wife, and one free woman of color would have worked to handle a range of domestic tasks alongside the enslaved women, like Ester and Charlotte, on the farm. The Black women who lived with Francis would have been moved between domestic labor and fieldwork as needed. Enslaved and free men on the farm labored in Francis's fields cultivating cotton and probably corn, a common supplementary crop. And youths such as his enslaved laborers Nathan, Tom, and Davy would have served as supplemental labor where needed.

In 1831, Berry Newsom, a free Black apprentice to Peter Edwards, was arrested and tried for alleged participation in the Southampton Rebellion.[28] His status as a free person of color bound out to a white master was not unusual in antebellum Southampton County.[29] Southampton's landowners used diverse labor sources to run their farms, and free people of color, including free children, supplemented the labor of the enslaved. Some of the county's substantial population of free Black people owned land or at least lived as part of households headed by a free Black person. Most free adults, though, lived on white-owned farms. By 1830, around 100 free people of color, many of them children, lived in the neighborhood that was most affected by the Southampton Rebellion.[30]

Berry Newsom lived on Peter Edwards's farm. His master owed most of his enslaved labor force to an advantageous marriage he had made in 1817 to the widow Nancy Bittle, which brought approximately fifteen enslaved people to his farm.[31] By 1830, Edwards enslaved thirty people. Eight of the thirty enslaved laborers he held were under the age of 10 and another thirteen were below the age of 24. Even if those in the latter category were primarily enslaved people who were closer to age 24 than to age 10, Edwards had only seven full experienced hands on his place. Hiring supplemental labor would not have been extravagant of Edwards.[32]

Enslaved adults of their home farms would have been charged with training young and less experienced hands. Children and youths required training to work in cotton fields and do many other tasks and chores on a farm. Rearing very young children and training older children was a type of labor for the adults on each place. Both white and Black adults who lived on small farms would have assigned the children daily chores and supervised their completion. Training and supervision took place during the workday as adults completed their own work. Aged women and young girls (who sometimes were very young) watched over the smallest children while adult men and women saw to the training of those that entered the workforce at age 6.[33] As they grew older, children and youths worked in closer proximity to adults in the fields. It did not matter if adults and children were blood relations, fictive kin, or merely tolerant of each other; the gang system that existed on a much smaller scale on small to midsized farms required them to interact during the working day. These moments of contact between generations were valuable sites of knowledge transfer. From the adults around them, children learned how to survive the often taxing pace of work and the violent methods enslavers used to coerce labor from their enslaved property.[34]

Children were well aware of the possible punishment for completing tasks incorrectly and often suffered harsh treatment from overseers and enslavers. Often the realities of brutal punishment was their first introduction to learning to survive and resist. Rev. W. P. Jacobs, formerly enslaved in Virginia, remembered his grandmother's stories about growing up and struggling to meet her enslaver's demands. When she could not pick the required amount of cotton, older enslaved people would sometimes top her off, but, he remembers, "Lots of times she would come up short and would have to take the whipping. . . . Grandma said that often she was whipped until she could barely grunt."[35] While older enslaved people modeled how to help those who could not make weight, they could not always help Jacobs's grandmother escape beatings. She in turn passed on the method of evading punishment and the memory of slavery's brutality to her grandson. The enslaved modeled how to survive and resist in the context of their daily labor regime and taught younger generations those skills.

Children often confronted the cruelty of the labor regime on their own. Simon Stokes remembered his childhood and the childhood of other enslaved children as full of work in "de co'n and de terbaccer and cotton fields."[36] Stokes, who was tasked with picking worms off tobacco plants, feared his overseer. He remembered him as "de means ole hound you're ever seen." His overseer often forced him to eat the worms he missed as he moved through the tobacco field. Stokes remembered preferring that punishment to the alternative, "three lashes on yo' back wit his ole lash . . . wusser dan bittin' de worms, fer yo' could bite right smart qick, and dat wuz all dat dar wuz ter it; but dem lashes done last a pow'full long time."[37] Stokes was not the only enslaved child forced to eat worms. Another formerly enslaved person, possibly named Nancy Williams, remembered that when she missed the vermin as she moved through tobacco rows, her enslaver "picked up a hand full of worms, he did, an' stuffed 'em inter my mouth." She noted that "Lordy knows how many of dem shiny things I done swallered, but I sho' picked em off careful arter dat."[38] Both had vivid memories of their enslaved childhoods that included their lives as laborers at very young ages. Both also remembered that learning to complete their chores and tasks correctly became one way to avoid punishment and survive their time in the fields.

Through their labor, children and youths also learned how to navigate the power structures that white adults maintained around them. Young people who encountered harsh lessons about the high cost of resistance in every aspect of their lives watched adults and learned which resistive practices were the riskiest and which could slip past their enslaver's notice. They learned through their own experiences, often while laboring, how to resist slavery on their own because they knew that Black adults could not always protect them. Children and youths in the African American communities of Southampton learned their place in the fields, outbuildings, and social structures of their communities every day. Long before the Southampton

Rebellion began, each of the boys and youths that adult rebels chose to take with them would have gleaned valuable knowledge of survival practices as they labored. But more than gleaning survival strategies, enslaved children trained to resist slavery.

Individuals who were raised in slavery, such as Nathan, Tom, Davy, and Moses, retained clear memories of their lives as enslaved children. Their memories of constant labor, harsh punishments, and the pervasive fear they experienced as children did not fade in old age. Those who were interviewed as part of the Works Progress Administration's (WPA) project to record the memories of the formerly enslaved in Virginia often related stories about older relatives and caretakers. This means that older enslaved people related to them, by narrating their experiences, what behavior to be careful of, how to survive severe beatings, and which actions led to death.[39]

The consequences that both adults and children suffered when they were caught defying their masters' authority left deep impressions on enslaved children. Allen Crawford grew up partially on the farm of Peter Edwards, the same farm where Berry Newsom had served years before the Southampton Rebellion as an apprentice. He was well aware of the history of resistance that surrounded him as a child. He recalled that he was "bred and born and reared within three miles of Nat Turner's insurrection—Travis Place."[40] He noted that his uncle Henry was hanged for participating in the rebellion.[41] As an elderly man, he could remember the exact patrol schedule in the county and details about how enslaved people in Southampton County evaded the patrols: "Law yes! I know something about the patrollers. There were three sets of dem in slavery working like shifts."[42] While he remembered that "I never went to none of dem meetings," Crawford still recalled the full schedule of patrols and remembered how to avoid them. That was particularly important information, given the consequences he outlined for being caught.

As a child, Crawford lived on a farm where at least one convicted rebel once lived and remembered that "dem meetings" still occurred and that apparently Black residents of the neighborhood still used practices to subvert local white authorities after the rebellion despite the possible consequences. Moses and the other young people charged with rebellion would have known well how power operated around them and would have had access to information about violence that was similar to what Crawford described.

The violent coercion that whites enacted to extract labor from Black people defined the lives of children like Nathan, Tom, Davy, Moses, and Berry Newsom. Children made no mistake about what defying white authority could mean for them. Fannie Berry, who came from Appomattox County, remembered that "when uh slave ud run away, ef dey catched him dey would 'punch and gag an' double quick' 'em all de way back home."[43] Katie Blackwell Johnson, who came from Washington County, in the far southwest corner of Virginia, remembered how she was punished. "Me? Yes, I got plenty of whippings 'cause I was full of mischief but they never cut my skin." She noted how violent her enslaver was to an elderly enslaved man: "Old 'Uncle' Lewis was caught stealin' hogs and chickens so often and whipped so much—I declare when he went to Gawd he didn't have the skin he was borned with."[44] This graphic memory demonstrates how aware children were of the violent punishments whites used to discipline enslaved adults and children. Free children also learned very quickly that free status did not protect them from white violence. Children also confronted the reality that whites punished Black people for what they perceived to be threats to their authority. Free-born Mollie Booker recalled, "De paddy rollers use to bother my father somepin' awful. Dey'd come an' beat him anytime."[45]

Enslaved and free children learned through their parents' modeling how to aid both members of their community and those who were passing through as truants and runaways. West Turner, who came from Nansemond County due east of Southampton County, remembered the story of his aunt Sallie, who went truant after one of their enslavers accused her of harming the white children in her care. "Pa used to put food in a pan 'neath de wash bench 'side de cabin, an' it was so dark Ant Sallie come on inside to eat it."[46] As a child he remembered hearing her dramatic escape from his family's cabin in detail from the loft where he slept at night:

> Ant Sallie ain't ketched yet. She grabbed up a scythe knife f'om de corner an' she pulled de chock out dat do' an' come out a-swingin'. . . . She cut her way out, den turned roun' and backed off into de woods, an ole Marsa was just screamin' an' cussin'.[47]

As a child, West Turner had a front-row seat to the strategies both his father and his aunt used to resist and survive. His father aided his aunt while she was truant and his aunt took a violent stand right in front of his family's cabin. These moments of crisis, resistance, and survival stuck with him well into his twilight years.

In the early hours of the morning of August 22, 1831, Moses awoke to find his homeplace in turmoil. The white adults who enslaved him and the Black adults who had taken part in training and rearing him were all impacted by the first murders of the rebellion. Every white person on his farm was dead when Moses left with the group of adult men who moved on to their next target in the neighborhood. Later that same morning, Nathan, Tom, and Davy were present on their homeplace when their enslaver received the news that something horrible had happened on the Travis place. They were still at home when rebels arrived and murdered their overseer and two white toddlers in the front yard. They were there when the rebels charged into their master's attic looking for Lavinia Francis, only to miss her limp body that lay between the rafters, overcome by the heat. Will and Sam, two men they'd worked next to day after day, were among them. Ester and Charlotte, whom Lavinia Francis would later discover making a meal for rebels they fully expected to return, were also present. Like the adults on the Travis place, the adults on the Francis farm would have worked closely with all three. And just as with Moses, the adult rebels on the place decided that the boys had witnessed enough, had been trained enough, had seen resistance modeled enough to move on with the rebel band.[48]

Adults spoke to children about relatives and other adults who had resisted enslavement knowing full well the serious consequences that could result.[49] For this reason, adult rebels may have decided that boys should ride along with them. Had the boys who were taken prisoner after the Southampton Rebellion run errands and done other work typical of enslaved children, they could have been valuable assets who knew the county's geography in a different way than adults did. Keeping them close would also prevent them from warning whites of impending danger, using the paths and routes they may have been familiar with.

Children not only observed resistive activity and heard cautionary and instructive tales, they also actively participated in community resistance. Annie Wallace remembered helping her mother escape capture in Culpeper, Virginia. She remembered that before her mother left for secret gatherings, she would instruct her and her siblings to wait up and listen for her returning home. Her mother's starched petticoats made a distinctive noise: "And when we heard them petticoats apoppin' as she run down the path, we'd open the door wide and she would get away from the patteroll."[50] Like the enslaved boys and youths who would stand trial in Southampton, Wallace did not attend the illicit meeting adults held. But she was expected to aid her mother's escape when the time came. The four young people conscripted by adult male rebels would have experienced similar expectations even as the witnessed violent acts that may or may not have frightened them. Whether adults expected children and young people to participate in the rebellion or simply stay put so they wouldn't give the rebellion away, they expected their compliance and at least tacit support.

Free children also supported adults who suffered at the hands of violent whites. Mollie Booker, who was free in her girlhood, remembered that during one particularly brutal attack on her father, "Mom an' we all kids stood in de door an' cried. Don' know whether hit helped much er not but we all stood dere an' cried jes' de same."[51] While her mother's strategy and her part in it were much subtler than the experiences of West Turner and Annie Wallace in childhood, each interview recounted how children helped adults evade capture and demonstrated one way that adults integrated children into their strategies of resistance.

Nathan, Tom, Davy, and Moses would each have been well schooled in the dangers, trials, and consequences of disobedience that were ever present in enslaved life. Bringing them along would have made perfect sense to enslaved men who already knew them and had helped train them as laborers. Their presence among the rebels who made their way from farm to farm similarly made perfect sense to white officials. And county justices were well aware of each young defendant's value as a keen observer. Black children's observations of resistive strategies went hand in hand with their participation in resistive practices. Modeling was a way of teaching resistive praxis to younger generations. It was, after all, their potential as future insurgents that local officials considered when they held them and charged them as adults in the days after the rebellion ended.

Children in the Wake of Rebellion

On the morning of August 22, 1831, a small enslaved boy from the Travis farm appeared at the Francis farm with troubling news. His message was short: The whites on the Travis place were all dead. The enslaved of Southampton were in rebellion.[52] The humid August heat in Southside Virginia can be overwhelming. The growth cycle of local cotton inspired the lying-in season, a time before harvest when the cotton had outgrown weeds and daily fieldwork could slacken. It was the perfect time to slip away, to abscond, to plot. The men who began their rebellion at the Travis place had seized the opportunity that season provided. Two weeks later, another boy from the Travis farm, Moses, provided the primary testimony for the prosecution in the cases of Nathan, Tom, and Davy,[53] all enslaved by Nathaniel Francis. While history books say the rebellion ended on August 23, 1831, it dragged on into November for those held in Southampton's county jail. With Nat Turner at large, the rebellion remained alive. And the lives of five boys hung in the balance.

At the end of August, the rebels had finally reached the county seat their army had so desperately tried to gain control over. But instead of raising the county's armory and securing the town of Jerusalem, those who were still alive found themselves in Southampton County's jail. In 1831, the jailhouse was a small building that stood close to the courthouse in downtown Jerusalem. Fifty prisoners that included one woman and five young people were awaiting trial or interviews with the court on August 31, 1831, when the court began hearing criminal cases related to the Southampton Rebellion. In the weeks and months that followed the local militia's suppression of the Southampton Rebellion on August 23, local authorities reined in local white violence and insisted that suspected rebels be brought to justice through Virginia's legal channels. The final days of many of those who lived through the initial vigilante and militia violence and were captured were spent in the close air of the jail. September offers a slow creeping reprieve to summer's swelter each year on the Southside. But it is often well deep into October before the heat truly retreats. The jail must have been stifling at first. And then, suddenly, the executions began on September 5. Each prisoner who remained must have felt acutely the empty space left by those whom officials led off to the hanging tree. The absence of each missing body's contribution to the heat, stench, and wretched conditions of the close quarters would have provided relief and grief at once.

As they awaited trial, Nathan, Tom, Davy, and Moses coped with these extreme conditions of incarceration. We are not sure if Berry Newsom and the free men of color held for questioning were thrown in a cell with the enslaved suspects or if they were housed separately. But the open nature of the jail would not have prohibited communication. There is no record of what prisoners spoke about while they were held in jail. We do not know if the boys and youths sought out advice from the men who were jailed with them or if they had received instructions while traveling along the rebellion route. But we do know that men, mostly from the boys' neighborhood, many from the boys' home farms, men they'd grown up listening to and learning from, began to disappear into the courtroom on August 31, the first day of hearings.

In the first week of trials, local justices handed down thirteen guilty verdicts that carried death sentences. Three men were given reprieve while they awaited the possibility of the governor's mercy: the possibility that they would be sold to work in the cotton fields of the Deep South instead of being executed. By the fourth day of trials, men who were enslaved with the boys on the Travis place and the Francis farm began to stand trial. Sam, whom Nathaniel Francis enslaved, and Hark, whom Joseph Travis enslaved, had returned to the jail with execution dates and no hope of reprieve.[54]

In the interim between the boys' capture and their court date, both defense lawyers and prosecutors for the commonwealth of Virginia interviewed them. They also interviewed Berry Newsom.[55] Moses was the most useful witness of the lot. But all of them were subjected to interviews and their testimony was heard in court; usually their lawyer read it to court justices.[56] The boys may have already known how the court of oyer and terminer, a special court for enslaved people, functioned. Enslaved Virginians were no strangers to the commonwealth's justice system. The boys could also have learned from fellow prisoners who had already stood trial what they could expect when they moved from the jailhouse to the courthouse. Because they were enslaved, they would have no jury. Instead, the attorney for the commonwealth and counsel for the defense brought evidence, called witnesses, and presented their case to justices of the peace in a court of oyer and terminer. The justices then passed judgment, either convicting a defendant or acquitting and releasing them. If the justices deemed the defendant worthy of mercy, they had the option to remand the defendant to jail and request that the governor of Virginia change a death sentence to removal from the state.[57] By the time the first of the young defendants entered Southampton's courthouse on September 6, defendants before them had met each fate.

The day before the jailer took Nathan, Tom, and Davy to the courthouse for arraignment, the first of the executions ordered by the court had begun.

The jailer took two of the men they had been imprisoned with to the gallows on September 5, 1831.[58] The next day, the justices called for Nathan, Tom, and Davy to be brought to the stand. The charge each of the boys faced was the same one adult defendants faced: "consulting, advising and conspiring with divers other slaves to rebel and make insurrection and making insurrection and plotting to take the lives of divers free white persons citizens of this Commonwealth."[59] Moses's lawyer also read his testimony in the courtroom that day. Moses had valuable information about his three peers and the happenings at the Francis place that offered a possible reason for mercy.

White authorities turned to some of the Black children and youths who were present during the rebellion for damning testimony against suspected rebels. Moses and two other enslaved children, Daniel and Beck (sometimes called Becky), appeared as witnesses. Daniel testified in one trial and Beck's testimony was used in the cases of three men from neighboring Sussex County.[60] Local authorities sought to influence, train, and assert power over Black children in the courtroom. Enslaved children were also valuable property that could quickly appreciate in value. However, these children's testimonies adhered to some of the patterns of adult testimony, reflecting the longer tradition of court testimony as an African American strategy of resistance and survival.

Moses testified in five cases, sometimes for the prosecution and sometimes for the defense, even though the court had stipulated that this would not earn him clemency in his own case.[61] He was a witness for the prosecution in four trials, including those of Nathan, Tom, and Davy. In each testimony Moses gave for the prosecution, he corroborated that the defendant was present at a key site of the rebellion and either implied or stated that the defendant was an unwilling participant. Moses's testimony therefore demonstrates how court testimony could be used as a resistive strategy and how important children's accounts could be in trials.[62]

Moses also testified for the prosecution in the case of Jack, a man from his neighborhood who was enslaved by William Reese. Moses emphasized that Jack accompanied the rebels reluctantly. He began by noting that Jack was sick at the Travis farm and asked the rebels to leave him behind. Moses ended his account by saying that "—they made the prisoner [Jack] go with them."[63] Although the prosecution had called Moses to testify against Jack, he repeatedly presented Jack as present but unenthusiastic.

Moses's insistence on Jack's reluctance may or may not have been per-
jury, but he certainly emphasized it, describing Jack's illness in detail: he
said that Jack "complained of being sick and wanted to go home but Hark
would not let him go."[64] He said he first saw Jack that day with "his head
between his hands resting on his knees" and that he was "in the yard sick."[65]
Moses's testimony thus asserted that Jack did not want to accompany the
rebels. Although he was testifying for the prosecution, it is possible that
he was angling for leniency for a defendant he knew well. Jack had kinship
ties to the farm where Moses lived, and Moses was old enough to know
that his words had consequences. In Jack's case, the justices provided no
mercy: they refused to recommend that he be sold to the Deep South and
instead sentenced him to hang.[66]

Moses also testified for the defense in the trial of an enslaved man named
Nathan. Nathan's enslaver, Benjamin Blunt, was another victim of the rebellion. On September 6, 1831, both the prosecution and Nathan's defense called
only one witness. Both were children.[67] Daniel, an enslaved boy, testified
against Nathan. The two knew each other from their time in the Greensville
County Jail. We do not know why Daniel was being held in jail one county
to the west of Southampton County, but Nathan was being held there as a
runaway. Daniel testified that Nathan spoke about who and what had inspired
him to flee Southampton. He said that Nathan "had been present when the
murders were committed by the insurgents" and "had blood on his breeches
which he said he had told the white people was cider."[68]

Then Moses testified for the defense. He corroborated that Nathan was
present at the Whitehead place. And just as he testified in other cases,
Moses asserted that Nathan "went unwillingly—that he committed no
murder." He finished by stating that he thought that "[Nathan] had no opportunity to escape and remained with the insurgents till they dispersed."[69]
The justices ruled that Nathan was guilty. Both boys' testimonies confirmed
that Nathan had spent time with rebels, thus making it impossible for the
court to render any other verdict.[70] We lack evidence about how Daniel was
involved in the Southampton Rebellion; we only know of his role in Nathan's
trial. But white officials allowed the two boys to have significant roles in the
proceedings. Their testimony was used to convict a man and sentence him
to death. Regardless of the degree to which either one participated in the
violence of the rebellion, each certainly participated in the violence of its

aftermath. In this way, the court justices reclaimed the labor and lives of each boy, conscripting their experience to serve the prerogative of whites in power.

Testifying in the tinderbox that was Southampton County in the fall of 1831 required that one be mindful of errant sparks. Given the experience of the boys who appeared in court as enslaved people, there is no reason to believe that they were not aware of this danger. Moses's insistence that each defendant hesitated could have been his way of angling for mercy. Moses was probably not lying for the sake of other enslaved people; it is more likely that he was explaining the complex reactions of each defendant. Hesitating was a sign of humanity, not an indication of allegiance to whites. In addition, survival was a primary goal for Southampton's enslaved people, even during a slave rebellion. Moses also knew that these trials determined the value of the defendants so their enslavers could be compensated if they were sentenced to death or sold out of state.[71] While Moses testified for the prosecution, he also noted the defendants' hesitance to join the rebellion and the fact that defendants needed to be coerced. Moses, in jail facing execution himself, was able to evaluate the stakes and provide evidence that served the prosecution but might also help keep his neighbors alive.[72]

The court heard Nathan, Tom, and Davy's cases as one case. The justices also carefully accounted for the three boys' ages. Their trial record reads, "it appeared that the oldest was not more than 15 years, the other two much younger, the oldest very badly grown."[73] The court clerk recorded these details about their appearance in service to their valuation as property. A badly grown fifteen-year-old would not command the same price at market as a healthy one. But this notation of their ages also suggests that the boys' youth complicated the possibility of convicting and executing them.[74] Their trial did not yield any testimony that any of them had been directly responsible for or involved in the murder of a white person. And the testimony heard for and against them did not suggest that they had attended meetings where adults plotted to rebel. Instead, the prosecution's case against Nathan, Tom, and Davy relied on using the testimony of another youth to demonstrate that they had been near the rebels.

Keeping in mind their experience in a community of laborers, their daily proximity to adults involved in the rebellion, and the rebels' deliberate plans to include them, the court appearances of the three young defendants offer an opportunity to think beyond their guilt or innocence and their enslavers' claims for compensation. Their cases, and those of the other young people who were tried that fall, offer an opportunity to investigate how children could have played a role in violent rebellion. The only evidence against Nathan, Tom, and Davy was that they rode along with adult rebels during the rebellion.

Moses's testimony reveals one way the adult rebels incorporated the boys into resistive practices. Whether the boys were willing or not, men older than them thought it best to bring them along. With Nathaniel Francis gone and his mother and wife nowhere to be seen, adult rebels who arrived on the Francis place made easy work of the remaining whites. They killed Francis's young overseer and his two orphaned nephews before picking up the young recruits. Moses said of his peers that "the three prisoners were taken from Nathl. Francis and placed one behind each of the company [and] that they went unwillingly." The rebels put them on horseback, each behind a rider. Moses testified that the three witnessed a number of murders but that they were held at gunpoint by older rebels who threatened to kill them if they tried to escape. They were not willing participants in the rebellion, in other words. But the prosecution only wanted to confirm that the boys were present when the rebels arrived at their homeplace and whether they then rode along with them.[75]

All three knew the adult men who forced them to ride along and who charged them with the labor of at least bearing witness to the violence that would unfold. After visiting the Francis place, the rebels visited at least nine farms, killing over thirty whites.[76] While it is possible that the men were mostly concerned about the boys' ability to warn whites, the boys were also old enough to have worked alongside some of the men. It is hard to imagine that they had not done so with Sam, who lived on the Francis farm with them. If the boys were old enough to learn farm labor, were they not also old enough to learn the labor of rebellion? It is impossible to know how the boys felt about being included or the rebels' true motivation for forcing them to mount up. But the men's experience with training male youths and children must have made them aware of what the three could accomplish. Adult male rebels ascertained that commandeering their labor, if only to ensure their silence and govern their mobility, was important. At the same time, adult rebels were not blind to the age of the three; they paired each with an adult for their journey. The men had considered the boys' ages and experience level and decided to keep them close.

Their closeness to adults proved to be the most bothersome issue for Southampton's justices. Nathaniel Francis was the enslaver of both Will, one of Nat Turner's key lieutenants, and Sam. Both were present at the Cabin Pond meeting where the rebellion began. Francis was also the enslaver of Dred, who joined the rebels when they visited the Francis place.[77] By the time the boys took the stand, Will had died during the rebellion, justices had tried and convicted Sam, and Dred was in their custody.[78] The boys had been raised, at least in part, by some of the most central figures in the Southampton Rebellion, including Charlotte and, more recently, Ester. The information that Sam had participated early in 1831 in planning the rebellion, that he had attended the meeting at Cabin Pond and had helped decide to launch the rebellion, and that he was close to Nat Turner was not included in the record of his trial.[79] It appears that in the cases of the boys they knew, Southampton's justices felt that witnessing murder under the tutelage of adult rebels posed a threat to local order and the slave system. Although the justices noted the three boys' youth and perhaps Moses's insistence that "that they went unwillingly," they pronounced the three young defendants guilty as charged and sentenced them to public hanging.[80]

Proximity to adult rebels proved sufficient for the court. In truth, whites in Southampton County and beyond would not have been satisfied with a verdict of not guilty. Such a verdict would have allowed the boys to remain in the county and, at least publicly, escape punishment. Although they were appointed as arbiters of justice, local magistrates remained accountable to their community. A guilty verdict demanded a death sentence and they handed one down for each defendant. They then chose to show their version of mercy.[81] They recommended that the governor of Virginia commute their sentences to expulsion from the state. According to Virginia law, this would stay Nathan, Tom, and Davy's executions until the governor decided to commute or uphold their sentences. If the governor decided to commute their executions, local officials would send the boys to Richmond to await sale. This was the ultimate fate that awaited the three when the court recommended that the governor commute their sentences to sale from the state. Local officials were well aware that showing mercy would bolster their claim that those who were hanged were executed justly and that power once again rested in the appropriate hands in Southampton County. Commuting a sentence to transfer also had the potential to recover some of the money the commonwealth had spent to reimburse enslavers for the loss of their human property.

For the three boys, this "mercy" was a social death sentence. Sale to a slave trader, who would almost certainly take them to the Deep South, meant permanent removal from home and all that was familiar. They would likely be split apart from each other. Davy, who suffered from stunted growth that may have been due to malnourishment, childhood illness, or a genetic condition, was particularly vulnerable. Beyond the physical hardships of life in a slave coffle, which often meant physical death, being sold from the enslaved community, family, and friends who had raised them would have been overwhelmingly painful and traumatic. Having the sentences of young boys commuted to sale away from Virginia would have been merciful only to the consciences of local magistrates.[82]

On September 20, 1831, local justices examined Berry Newsom, a free Black apprentice to Peter Edwards.[83] Southampton County's local court could not try free people of color suspected of involvement in the rebellion. Under Virginia law, involvement in a slave rebellion was a capital crime. Free people of color charged with involvement in a slave rebellion had to be tried by the circuit superior court, which met less frequently than the local court, which typically met once a month. While local authorities held significantly more court sessions to accommodate the volume of trials after the rebellion, the higher court did not convene until the spring of 1832. The presiding justices had to be content with holding hearings for free people of color that determined whether to remand suspects to jail to await trial at the next superior court or to release them. In all, the county court held hearings for five people of color, four men and one youth.

Extant documents note only that the hearing took place and do not provide any details about Newsom's interview. Some evidence of Newsom's involvement appears in the trial of Hardy, who was enslaved by Benjamin Edwards, on September 7, 1831. From Hardy's testimony, it is evident that Newsom helped bury the dead on the Waller farm, a site of extensive carnage, after the rebellion ended. Hardy also said that Newsom was enthusiastic about the rebellion before it took place.[84] According to an account of what Hardy testified, "Berry stated that the damned Rascal, meaning the witness' master, had been there, that they would get him before night."[85] After Newsom's hearing, the justices remanded him to await further trial. Later in the spring of 1832, the superior court sentenced him to death.[86]

Berry Newsom was the only free youth of color who was tried and executed for his role in the rebellion. It is impossible to know from his case
alone if other free children and youths of color shared his enthusiasm for
the rebellion. He was one of many bound youths in the county at the time.
He was about the age of Nathan, Tom, Davy, and Moses. Although he did
not act on his feelings, he spoke the language of rebellion and suffered
death for it. His defiance of the racial hierarchy as a free person of color was
apparently more egregious to Virginian authorities than the roles enslaved
boys played in the rebellion.

Justices initially charged Moses in late August 1831, but they delayed his
trial after realizing his usefulness as a witness. His access to rebels and the
events of the rebellion ensured his value on the stand. Moses joined the
adult rebels at his homeplace, the Travis farm, and remained with them at
least until they visited the Turner place. He was also present on the Francis
farm on the first morning of the rebellion, where he joined the rebels again.
He remained with rebels until militia scattered them at Parker's Field on
August 22.[87]

Moses's trial on October 18, 1831, was the last one before officials captured and tried Nat Turner in November. Moses's experience with rebels
and with the Southampton County courts suggests that he engaged in
active resistance. The justices heard "divers witnesses" for the prosecution
who attested to Moses's guilt and used his own testimony against him.
Jeff Drewry, who was "present on several occasions when the prisoner was
examined as a witness on previous trials," said that Moses's "evidence was
given freely and voluntarily after being told he was not compelled to give
testimony & nothing which he said would be of any advantage to him."[88]
Moses testified in other trials with the full knowledge that his words would
not protect him. Although "he had been compelled to go with the insurgents," an insistence that he was reluctant was not a part of his formal
defense.[89] He would have had an idea of how difficult his case would be to
win. He lost members of his community through his experiences during
the rebellion and his participation in court proceedings. It is important to
note that given the scope of his losses, his experience watching neighbor
after neighbor disappear from the jailhouse, and the guilty verdicts he'd
had a hand in, Moses pleaded not guilty, even though he knew how hard it
would be to win an acquittal.

On October 18, 1831, the court convicted Moses and sentenced him to death by hanging but recommended that his sentence be commuted to sale from Virginia.[90] And so, valued at $300, Moses became one of the missing hands and missing faces in Southampton County.[91] He was one of the last to disappear from the jail and into the uncertainty of the internal slave trade of the early antebellum South.

On October 30, 1831, weeks after Moses stood trial, a local farmer discovered Nat Turner in a dugout cave very near Cabin Pond and the Travis place. Justices tried Turner on November 5, 1831. After delivering a swift guilty verdict, they remanded Turner to jail to await execution on November 11, 1831.[92] With his capture and hanging, many whites pronounced that the rebellion was over. White officials used the court system to quell the fears of the white public. They even managed to demonstrate their version of civility through acts of mercy. They also effectively used court proceedings to reestablish, preserve, and project their mastery. Although executing Black children was by no means off limits, the justices of the county court may have felt that the four young people were too young to be held accountable for the decisions of adults. But perhaps the justices were in denial. Saying that enslaved children were easily influenced by the Black adults they knew would have been one way for the justices to project control. Children were the embodied future of slavery. If the justices had admitted that they could be willing rebels and participants in the carnage, they would have been acknowledging that children actively endeavored to emancipate themselves. Purposeful rebellion on the part of enslaved children had to remain unimaginable for Southampton whites. Thus, recommending mercy while pronouncing guilt was a successful strategy for the justices to use, one that preserved their future dominance.

Only four of the hundreds of enslaved children present in the neighborhood that was home to the Southampton Rebellion stood trial. The governor commuted the sentences of all four to transfer from the state. Although these boys and youths disappeared, others were left behind to continue with chores, fieldwork, and labor. Others yet to be born, like Allen Crawford, would speak about the rebellion's impact on their lives into the twentieth century.[93] While whites struggled to suppress memories of the event, African Americans in Virginia continued to talk about Nat Turner's legacy in a local colloquialism. Cornelia Carney remembered from her childhood that adults would say, "White folks was sharp too, but not sharp enough to git by ole Nat." She explained that "ole folks used to say it all de time. De meaning' I git is dat de n——s could always out-smart de white folks."[94] And so children would carry the importance of the Southampton Rebellion into the future in their memories of past generations.

Analyzing the roles that children played in African American communities in the antebellum South, as laborers in proximity to adults and as trial witnesses, brings a deeper understanding of the Southampton Rebellion. Free or enslaved, the children and youths of Southampton County were important to the event and to its traumatic aftermath. It is clear from the trials of Nathan, Tom, Davy, and Moses that adult male rebels decided to bring them along. Each witnessed violence and each suffered being severed from their community through transport after the rebellion. Whether they were rebels or witnesses, neither Black nor white adults overlooked them in the local context of the rebellion. Their role in their community involved observing adults as they resisted slavery.

The memories of African American children who had grown up in Virginia during the antebellum era and the evidence in trial records of five young people who witnessed the rebellion begin to illuminate the complex relationship of enslaved and free children to resistance. The courtroom appearances of a handful of children and youths reveal that enslaved adults and white adults believed they were critical to the rebellion and its aftermath. Whether they did so intentionally or unintentionally, voluntarily or because they were coerced, African American children witnessed and participated in local resistance. Oral histories of adults who were enslaved as children contextualize the experiences of those on trial in Southampton. Some could only describe proximity to adult actions, but others clearly remembered actively participating in community resistance. It is important to acknowledge the place and role of children in Southampton County and to further explore the role they may have played in community resistance. Through their potential to labor, they embodied future wealth for enslavers. The men who fomented the Southampton Rebellion were also thinking of the future. To them, African American children embodied the future of resistance. In the wake of the rebellion, Black children continued to feature in geographies of both surveillance and control even as they contributed to newly developing geographies of evasion and resistance.

5

Surviving Southampton

Geographies of Survival

Sir,—You have asked me to give a history of
the motives which induced me to undertake
the late insurrection, as you call it—To do
so I must go back to the days of my infancy,
even before I was born.

—Nat Turner, quoted in *The Confessions of
Nat Turner and Related Documents*

By the end of 1831, local officials had executed eighteen enslaved men and one enslaved woman: Daniel, Moses, Nat, Nelson, Hark, Davy, Sam, Nathan, Jack, Joe, Lucy, Davy, Dred, Curtis, Stephen, Ben, Sam, and Nat Turner. They'd asked the governor to sell Andrew, Isaac, Jack, Nathan, Tom, Davy, Hardy, Isham, and Moses out of the state. Add to that the twenty-two extralegal killings that included putting heads at the crossroads long known as Black Head Signpost.[1] Death enveloped the county. There is no limit to bereavement, no moment when a person stops surviving the dead. The militia response, the trials, the sentences, and the community that circulated through the geography of surveillance and control in the county seat of Jerusalem changed Southampton forever. As harvest time came and went, the absence of missing laborers and missing kin was conspicuous.

But even after Nat Turner had been captured and executed, whites were not able to fully quell their nagging anxiety.[2] Although enslaved and free

African Americans had mapped new ways of surviving, they confronted the reality every day that survival is also a synonym for grief.

The rebellion had taken only two days, from the early hours of August 22 through August 23. The trials and executions went on for months. The group of enslaved men who gathered with Nat Turner at Cabin Pond on the night of August 21 swelled to an estimated fifty or more enslaved and free men and boys. They murdered fifty-five white men, women, and children in quick succession, gathering weapons and insurgents as they went. At the Travis place, they murdered Nat Turner's enslaver and his entire family, including an infant. They targeted whites in their own neighborhood whom they knew well.

Ultimately, a chance encounter with militia at Cypress Bridge and the disorganization that followed undid what had been a lethal revolt until the afternoon of August 22. White retaliatory violence was swift and bloody. Militia members placed the heads of suspected rebels on pikes; they tied Charlotte, enslaved by Nathaniel Francis, to a tree and executed her at Cross Keys; and they took prisoners to Jerusalem to await trial. But still Nat Turner evaded them.[3]

To white residents of Southampton County, the most galling absence was that of Nat Turner. Local whites wondered how the leader of the rebellion was able to disappear and feared what he might be planning while he evaded capture. In the interest of restoring order, they worked to rebuild and maintain a geography of control and surveillance. To do so, they put their trust in local magistrates. In the late summer and fall of 1831, trial after trial, execution after execution, and day after day in the local jail, whites did their best to quell local fears and demonstrate their power over African Americans held in custody on suspicion of involvement in the rebellion. A court of oyer and terminer condemned men, boys, and even one woman to death. They also interviewed free people of color before they were tried in a higher court. All the while, cloaked in the silence of the Black community, Nat Turner remained at large. Whites found that even as public executions proceeded, local order and the peace were not assured.[4] At every turn, in every official deposition and interview, white officials were met with Black silence.

In late October 1831, after weeks of reports that Turner had been sighted in the area, a farmer named Benjamin Phipps and his dog found Nat Turner. Phipps's delivery of Turner to the authorities brought to an end the trials that began almost as soon as militia put an end to the rebellion. With Nat Turner in custody, whites finally felt they had put the rebellion down. While Turner was in jail, an attorney named Thomas R. Gray deposed him. Gray later sold Turner's deposition as *The Confessions of Nat Turner*.[5] The court found Nat Turner guilty as charged based on his confession and sentenced him to death by hanging.

It is easy to overlook the fact that *The Confessions of Nat Turner* are part of official court documentation. Gray published the document for profit, hoping to cash in on the fast-growing legend of America's most famous rebellious enslaved person. His entrepreneurial venture ensured that *The Confessions of Nat Turner* would go on to have a life of its own in the minds of generations of rebels and revolutionaries.[6] He also submitted Nat Turner's confessions to the court of oyer and terminer that convened on November 5, 1831, for Turner's trial and had it certified by the clerk of the district on November 10, the day before Turner's execution.[7] When the court asked Turner during his trial if there was any reason, given his confession, why he should not face hanging, Turner replied that "he had nothing further [to add] than [what] he had communicated to Mr. Gray." James Rochelle, the county clerk, entered his confession into the court record along with the court's death sentence.[8]

The extant record of the trials of those who were arrested after the uprising reveals how African American defendants and witnesses employed tactics of evasion and resistance. It is helpful to consider *The Confessions of Nat Turner* as one testimony among a community of testimonies by people who made the short walk from the county's crowded jailhouse to the courthouse. Read before a panel of justices at a court of oyer and terminer, these testimonies, which the county clerk recorded from memory in the county's minute books, offer glimpses of Black strategies and survival practices at a node of white patriarchal power. Turner's jailhouse confession should be understood in this context. His testimony demonstrates a shrewd instinct for community preservation in the face of death that is an instructive frame for the preceding testimonies of African Americans who faced justices.[9]

For Nat Turner, the story of his attempt to emancipate his community began with the legacy his parents and his grandmother left him. His mother and grandmother encouraged him to understand his worth outside slave schedules and slave sales. His sense of destiny, he recalled, also came from the community in which he grew up. His account of the rebellion reveals how important his neighborhood and his neighbors were to his decision to make his vision for freedom manifest.[10] Despite his odd behavior, his religious eccentricities, and his penchant for truancy, a small group of men met with him over the course of a year to plot and plan for the rebellion they carried out together.[11] They had relied on him in their youth to help them evade whites, and this attempt to save themselves and their kin from lives in bondage was an extension of that trust. Nat Turner said that "such was the confidence of the negroes in the neighborhood, even at this early period of my life, in my superior judgement, that they would often carry me with them when they were going on any roguery, to plan for them."[12] Turner's words throughout his confession attest to both his sense of purpose and the importance of the enslaved community for constructing and executing the plan to rebel.[13]

While Turner's confession provided valuable testimony about the events of the rebellion, it is also significant evidence of one of the most effective resistive tactics the enslaved community had: silence. Turner's omissions and silences were considerable. He did not mention a single enslaved person by name in connection with the rebellion whom officials had not already captured, tried, and executed. He divulged no details about his truancy before the rebellion. He gave no details about how he managed to live in a woodpile and two dugout caves in his own neighborhood for months. He remembered explicitly that he was "afraid of speaking to any human being."[14] It is hard to believe that he survived alone with no help from African Americans in the neighborhood where he was concealing himself.[15] In fact, two Black men made contact with Nat Turner before Benjamin Phipps discovered him by accident. Turner remembered that "two negros having started to go hunting" with a local dog discovered him and that he "spoke to them to beg concealment."[16] They offered him no such grace and reported him. This led Turner to abandon his first hiding place for a new dugout cave, where Phipps stumbled upon him two weeks later. Silence would have been powerful had the two men who found him stayed quiet.

To understand the courtroom actions and voices of enslaved and free African Americans, we must trust silence. It is important to acknowledge what the available sources cannot reveal. But it is also important to be clear that some silence in the extant archive signifies intent, agency, and strategy. Survival after the initial violence of the rebellion required those who remained, white and Black, to dissemble about certain truths while manufacturing a new status quo. That negotiation took place in the empty spaces in the fields and quarters of the county that those who were jailed or dead no longer filled—about what to speak, whom to accuse and charge, and when to remain silent. These were all choices that residents of Southampton across the color line mulled over and carefully considered. The courtroom in Jerusalem was a site of mastery, a site of state and local power, and a site of violence. But it was also a site of resistance, subversion, and survival.

Navigating the Court Proceedings: A Geography of Punishment and Incarceration

The trials that followed the Southampton Rebellion were not unique in their form or their function. Like courts convened for generations in Virginia, the court of oyer and terminer that tried suspected rebels was a theater where white males performed their mastery and executed their very real power over Black people's lives. These courts were embedded in long-standing cultural and legal tradition. Residents built the county's first courthouse when Virginia was still a colony. After independence from England, Jerusalem became the county seat of Southampton because of its importance to the county's legal history. It became the location where local criminal and civil courts convened and circuit court days took place.[17]

On court days, Jerusalem served as a gathering place where residents could socialize, share news from court proceedings, and make up their own minds about trial outcomes. In the early antebellum period, a courthouse, the surrounding grounds, and even the courtroom could be boisterous arenas for public participation in legal proceedings. Court days were social occasions and community events. It was not unusual for confrontations to take place outside the courtroom in response to rulings that crowds deemed unjust.[18]

In the fall of 1831, local officials faced a community that was frighteningly out of order to them. Enslaved people had managed to murder their neighbors and kin, and the scope of the rebellion was still unknown when trials began in Jerusalem. Turner's absence loomed. Regaining control, placing that control in the hands of the right sort of white men, and reestablishing hierarchical order was paramount. To that end, justices were tasked with trying as many suspects as were needed to restore the peace. As Patrick Breen points out in his assessment of the county court records,

"Firmly in control of the court's proceedings, Southampton's elite used the trial to promote their interpretation of the revolt: it was a small affair involving only a few slaves."[19] This narrative benefited the broader community of whites who were eager to know that both class and racial hierarchy had been restored. It behooved them to believe that most of their human property did not want them dead. And it benefited enslavers financially to execute and sell as few enslaved people as possible.

All of the justices who served in the county court were enslavers with considerable holdings.[20] Their status in the community made them eligible to serve as magistrates. Although some antebellum magistrates might have had legal training, a legal education was not a requirement. Instead, communities looked to white men they trusted to best keep the peace. As historian Laura Edwards notes, "Keeping the peace meant keeping everyone—from lowest to highest—in their appropriate places, as defined in specific local contexts."[21] The men who served as local magistrates were expected to know the community they served and to understand the unique needs of that community. They would have known how important enslaved labor was to each of their neighbors based on their experiences and relationships with them. They knew how much the value of each enslaved person shored up the finances of small and medium-sized farms in the county. As the harvest season approached, the rotating panel of justices who constituted the court needed to preserve an entire economic system to restore their own sense of the peace. Truly investigating the reach of the rebellion among the entire Black community was less of a priority for them than incarcerating an acceptable number of enslaved people in jail and controlling the narrative of the rebellion.[22]

The courthouse, the jailhouse, and the tree used for hangings made up the physical geography of incarceration and punishment at the heart of Jerusalem. Much like the geographies of surveillance and control white enslavers maintained, powerful whites built and used a geography of incarceration and punishment that consisted of very public venues to demonstrate their mastery to white and Black Southampton residents (see map 4). In 1831, the county jail was a small wood-frame building that was a few steps away from the courthouse in downtown Jerusalem. "The interior was divided into four cells, or 'apartments,' each enclosed by iron bars crossing at right angles and secured to the ceiling timbers."[23] Nearby, a tree along the main roadside served as gallows.

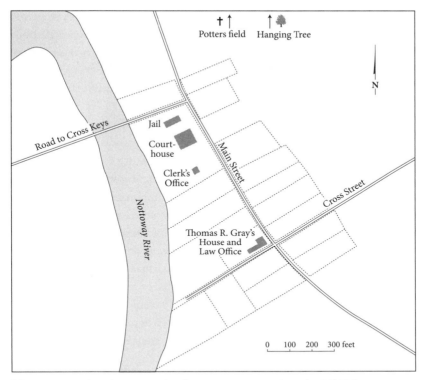

Potters field   Hanging Tree

N

Road to Cross Keys

Jail

Court-
house

Clerk's
Office

Main Street

Cross Street

Nottoway River

Thomas R. Gray's
House and
Law Office

0   100   200   300 feet

Map 4. Jerusalem (now Courtland), Virginia, in 1831. Map by Bill Nelson.

On September 5, 1831, when public executions began, trials continued and justices heard a full docket.[24] The sheriff, the justices, and, initially, the militia who captured suspected rebels and delivered them to Jerusalem worked together to substantiate the boundaries of the geography of incarceration and punishment. The broader community of white Southampton residents, including the most marginalized members, played an active role in maintaining and sustaining that geography. Both the Black and white communities of the county circulated in the space between the nodes of legal power within this geography—the jail, courthouse and courtroom, and the hanging tree.

Through almost all of the proceedings, Nat Turner remained truant, casting a pall of uncertainty. Local officials and white residents wanted expediency, closure, and mastery in a moment of uncertainty, ambiguity, and the most successful challenge to their power to date. By carefully defining and controlling venues of power, local officials, justices, and white residents did their best to project mastery and exert power. Black residents, both free and enslaved, wanted to survive white violence, evade white suspicion, and build new strategies of resistance to white reprisals. As they circulated through this public geography of incarceration, African Americans did their best to survive.

The militia delivered fifty Black people they suspected of involvement in the rebellion into the custody of the sheriff at the local jailhouse in late August. The jailhouse served a dual purpose in the life of the county after the rebellion. For the enslavers who sought to exercise control, the jailhouse was an essential part of their geography of incarceration. While it was not always common practice to hold suspects in custody in the 1830s, containing suspected rebels was of paramount importance. White officials expected that incarcerating suspected rebels would serve as a public demonstration of mastery. The suspects could not slip away to a meeting, visit with kin, or engage in any number of practices whites labeled as truancy like they might have when their enslavers surveilled them. With their lives hanging in the balance, those the sheriff held in custody were back under white control. As far as whites were concerned, that was an important step toward restoring the peace.

Local men of means who served as justices constituted a court of oyer and terminer, the type of court state law required for the trial of enslaved people for capital offenses. These courts did not include juries. However, the court assigned an attorney to each defendant; William C. Parker, James L. French, Thomas R. Gray, William B. Boyle, and Robert Burchett served as counsel for enslaved defendants.[25] The attorney for the commonwealth prosecuted those who were brought to trial.[26] Both the defense and prosecution presented their case to the court, based on evidence collected through deposing witnesses. African Americans served as witnesses for both the defense and prosecution. While whites strove to establish normalcy, African Americans assessed white motives and actions, awaited trial outcomes, and built a competing geography of evasion and survival.[27]

The jail, the courthouse, the courtroom, and the hanging tree served as landmarks in more than one geography. The courthouse and the courtroom were spaces of authority and real power over the lives of Southampton's white and Black residents. Justices had the ability to sentence defendants to death. They did so in the majority of the cases related to the rebellion.[28] But the courtroom was also a place for attorneys to argue their cases, for justices to hear them, and for the clerk to record the outcome. Both white and Black residents had defined and shaped this process over time in Virginia, and those who participated in the trials after the Southampton rebellion had inherited long-standing legal traditions and procedures. Southampton's white residents participated in the legal proceedings in multiple capacities: the sheriff, attorneys, and justices were all white men. The witnesses in many cases included both white men and women. White residents were familiar with the courthouse and the courtroom where magistrates heard their civil and criminal cases. The center of Jerusalem was familiar ground for whites, legally and socially.

Enslaved and free African Americans also occupied the geography of downtown Jerusalem. Although they were marginalized and subordinate under state law, they participated in the legal proceedings of their communities.[29] They participated in trials, although they could not bear witness against whites. They made claims and registered their status as free people of color. They interacted with local magistrates in both mundane civil matters and critical criminal cases.

Enslaved and free Black people also shaped new geographies of evasion, resistance, and survival. For the men and boys and the one woman who awaited trial and sentencing in the four rooms that made up cells, the local jail was a site of both incarceration and community. It is hard to imagine whites in Southampton sanctioning a meeting of nearly fifty enslaved people and a handful of free people of color in the heart of Jerusalem, but that is what they did when they put suspects in the crowded jailhouse. The first of the prisoners did not begin to disappear to the gallows until weeks after they arrived in Jerusalem.[30] In the interim, enslaved and free people attended their arraignments, were remanded to jail, stood trial, served as witnesses, and awaited execution. As they circulated within the geography of incarceration and punishment that the jail, the courthouse grounds, and the courtroom constituted, they gleaned valuable information, and in their cells they had ample time and motivation to communicate with each other.

Fleeting opportunities to communicate with those outside presented themselves as Black defendants circulated past onlookers on the courthouse grounds, as the sheriff took convicted rebels to the hanging tree for execution, and as those the court had granted a modicum of mercy moved off to Richmond for sale out of the state. Community members who were not held in custody also circulated in and out of the same spaces and took news back to their home farms and communities, linking the downtown community space with other communities all over the county.

Although whites sought a return to order and hierarchy, the space in downtown Jerusalem was not static and absolute. The court itself was changing and dynamic. From late August to November 1831, during eighteen court dates, the composition of panel of justices changed more than a dozen times. At times, the bench changed between trials. Although the legal proceedings were heavily weighted in favor of the power and interests of white enslavers, they also contained a small space for negotiation. Justices weighed the benefit to the peace and their conception of the natural hierarchy of the community as they evaluated each defendant's case and made their rulings. The courtroom did not subdue or flatten the personalities, histories, and connections of trial participants. The violence of the rebellion that spread across the county converged with the kinship ties, competing interests, and fears of white and Black residents. The rebellion had been an intimate one, and the context of the geography of the town of Jerusalem threw that intimacy into sharp relief: no longer scattered on farms out in the county, neighbors of all colors, both free and enslaved, faced each other in the courtroom, on public grounds, in the jailhouse, and at the hanging tree. All of Southampton's communities were determined to continue surviving the Southampton Rebellion. The extant record, although it is filtered through the clerk's memory and was created in service to the court's priorities, presents fragments of Black voices from the jailhouse where those who waited for their trials gave depositions and provides a window into how competing geographies formed and layered over time.

Contested Terrain:
Enslavers and the Court Proceedings

The members of society that built a legal system to serve their interests found limited success in court proceedings when they attempted to defend and thus retain ownership of the people they enslaved. For household after household, the rebellion had proved that the white men and women who were supposed to wield control over human property by defining what geography that property inhabited had failed. In many cases, in the absence of physical evidence that an enslaved defendant had participated in a specific murder, the prosecutor relied on evidence that a defendant had been away from the farm of their enslaver. Overwhelmingly, the living owners of enslaved defendants met with defeat when they attempted to advocate for their human property. As Laura F. Edwards explains, "even the wealthiest, most powerful community leaders held their positions at the behest of the public order; their authority was contingent on accepting and fulfilling their own obligations within the social order. When they failed in their duties, others could invoke the interests of the peace to discipline them."[31] The court had authority over the people whites considered property in part because the patriarchs, and occasional matriarchs, who should have controlled them had failed to keep the community safe from slave rebellion. It was now up to the court to take up the responsibility of disciplining the unruly enslaved people who murdered white residents, upending the power structure of the county.

The justice that could be found in Southampton County still benefited white people and the system within which they built wealth derived from enslaved labor. But enslavers navigated the geography of punishment that the courtroom, the jail, and the gallows constituted on different terms than those with which they navigated the geographies of surveillance and control on their farms. They had failed to properly control and surveil enslaved people who labored for them, and as a result, their neighbors and kin were dead. Enslavers found their authority changed in the courtroom as the result of the extraordinary context of slave rebellion.

Enslavers took seriously the requirement that they rely on the court to punish, execute, or sell those they considered their human property when enslaved people stepped outside the boundaries of their farms. Over generations, white men had built a legal system that upheld their interests as enslavers. For the most part, this system left punishment of enslaved people to the discretion of individual enslavers. In the case of a violent revolt, the law protected whites who participated in a community effort to put a rebellion down. Whites could not be held accountable for killing, injuring, or disciplining enslaved people they apprehended during a rebellion. Trials were important to those who enslaved suspected rebels. The justices who presided over each case were all white men of a class position similar to the enslavers who stood to lose both the labor and monetary value of their enslaved property held in custody.

The trials vested power in the class of white men at the top of the social hierarchy of the community, men who could be counted on to preserve power relations. The militia, which consisted of white men of all classes who were of an age to serve in the military, was the white community's first line of defense.[32] They had put the rebellion down. Although they had killed enslaved people, their brand of violent justice did not serve the long-term interest of enslavers. Without trials, enslavers had no redress or hope for compensation for executed human property. Given that most of the enslaved people held in custody were men of an age to be full hands, the financial loss after the rebellion had the potential to be considerable to individual enslavers. Although they ceded their power over their human property in extreme cases, they knew that the court was still invested in preserving the place of enslavers in race and class hierarchies.[33]

Enslavers who survived the rebellion appeared at the courthouse to testify both for and against enslaved defendants. Some of them had barely escaped death during the rebellion, others had lost numerous family members, and all had a financial interest in how court proceedings played out. Others participated in the trials of their own enslaved laborers. Most knew the justices; some were related by blood or marriage to them. Others were related to or acquainted with the attorneys who argued for and against enslaved defendants. The behavior of enslavers in court, the testimonies they gave during trials, and their relationships to local justices illuminate some important features of the geography of incarceration and punishment of the legal system.[34]

On the first day of court proceedings, four justices arraigned six enslaved people before beginning their first criminal case. The docket would ultimately prove to be too much as the day wore on. The court had to remand some defendants to jail for trial on a later date. They began with Daniel, a man enslaved by Richard Porter. Daniel and the other enslaved people on the docket faced charges of "feloniously counseling, advising and conspiring with each other and divers other slaves to rebel and make insurrection and making insurrection and taking the lives of divers free white persons of the Commonwealth."[35] Daniel was not on trial for a specific murder or murders. He was on trial for the entire rebellion at once, from plot to execution, as was the case with many after him. As with the many trials to follow, the prosecution did not bring evidence of Daniel's participation in specific murders or plotting. Instead, the attorney for the commonwealth relied on witnesses who could provide evidence that Daniel had strayed from his enslaver's property and had been in proximity to known murders or rebels. Richard Porter, Daniel's enslaver, survived the rebellion and provided testimony in Daniel's defense. Porter's participation and the outcome of Daniel's trial provide information about the dynamics of the court.

The justices used Daniel's case to state and record key information. Nathaniel Francis testified to the existence of a slave rebellion in Southampton. He stated "that a number, say between 50 and 60 free white persons were murdered / on / Sunday night the 21st & Monday morning the 22d of August 1831 by a number of negroes . . . and it was generally believed that there was insurrection among the negroes of the county."[36] The attorney for the commonwealth wanted to formally present the court with evidence that the charges against Daniel and the other men that day were well founded. Local officials wanted to establish that the prisoners brought to trial were part of a large conspiracy to foment violent rebellion. The kin of some of those rebellion victims provided testimony against Daniel that placed him well outside the geography of surveillance and control of the Porter place during the rebellion. The facts that he was near the rebels and spent time away from the control of Richard Porter shored up the prosecutor's case.

Daniel's trial involved a number of white witnesses. Levi Waller identified Daniel as one of the men present when his wife was murdered, testifying that he "saw the prisoner Daniel & two other negroes / named Aaron and Sam / go into a log house where the witnesses wife / and a small girl / had attempted to seacrete [sic] themselves."[37] Another white male witness, Sampson C. Reese, testified that Daniel had participated in the rebellion at various locations. He testified that he "shot at the prisoner [Daniel]," although he also noted that Daniel appeared to be unarmed.[38] Neither witness could confirm that Daniel had committed murder. They could only substantiate his involvement with and proximity to rebellion activities. Proximity and presence outside white geographies of surveillance and control proved to be enough to convict many suspects in later trials.

Richard Porter then offered testimony in Daniel's defense. Porter was a prominent man. He enslaved thirty people and lived in a stately two-story home at the time of the rebellion. He was one of the few landowners in the neighborhood who approached genteel status.[39] Porter testified that "he was told the prisoner [Daniel] had surrendered himself," adding that Daniel "was at home Monday morning" and that he "saw nothing uncommon about the prisoner."[40] As far as Porter was willing to testify, Daniel had been on his place the Monday of the rebellion and had given himself over into custody without resisting capture. Richard Porter may have intended to punish Daniel on his own. He may have thought that Daniel had been coerced, given that he acted normally after the rebellion was over. Or he may have wanted to avoid losing a prime male hand. Porter had many possible motivations for speaking on behalf of Daniel. Most important, he was a white man who had lived through the chaos of the rebellion. Advocating for his own property in a venue designed to rule in his favor was financially and socially prudent.

Despite Porter's testimony, justices decided to rule Daniel guilty and sentence him to "be hanged by the neck until he be dead."[41] These words would echo in the courtroom over the next few months. But it was the last time it was heard that day. Daniel's execution date was set for Monday of the next week. The justices valued Daniel at a mere $100. The court recognized Richard Porter's place in community hierarchies as an enslaver and a landowner by compensating him for his financial loss. But the money the court gave Porter could not help with the harvest season that loomed. Porter would have missed Daniel's labor and his value at auction. Additionally, Porter had to accept the court's authority to take the life of a person he enslaved and deny him the right to discipline his own human property. Despite all of Porter's privilege and standing in the community, his appearance at the courthouse did nothing to mitigate the damage his inability to confine Daniel to his farm had done.

Of the six prisoners the court arraigned that day, the justices considered the cases of only three additional enslaved people after Daniel. The justices decided to remand Moses, enslaved by Thomas Barrow, and Jack, enslaved by Catharine Whitehead, who died during the rebellion, back to jail. Although they considered the case of Tom, another of Catharine Whitehead's enslaved laborers, that day, the clerk did not record Tom's trial. The record simply notes that he pled not guilty and that the court heard testimony on his behalf. The justices found Tom not guilty and discharged him from custody.[42]

The court cared about the rights and privileges of individual enslavers, living and deceased, but they cared more about reinforcing their control and mastery over the county's Black population. If enslavers could not control their enslaved laborers, the court would step in to preserve the peace. In the absence of physical evidence, established proximity to rebels and murders were enough for the court to convict and sentence enslaved people to death. In trial after trial, mobility would prove to be the damning evidence against enslaved defendants.

Other enslavers testified in trials involving people they enslaved. Jacob Williams testified against Nelson, a member of his enslaved labor force. Likewise, Peter Edwards appeared to testify in defense of Sam. One white woman, Mary Barrow, who was widowed during the rebellion, appeared at the courthouse to testify in the case of Lucy, the only enslaved woman tried for participation in the rebellion. In each case, the justices handed down guilty verdicts.[43]

The verdicts tell only one dimension of the story of enslavers' involvement in the cases of people they enslaved. Richard Porter and Peter Edwards attested to the character of the people they enslaved. Porter testified that Daniel had turned himself in and displayed the proper amount of deference to him after the rebellion. Peter Edwards testified that Sam "was a negro of good character." Both also noted that the two men in question were back on their farms at reasonable hours on the Monday of the rebellion. Edwards testified "that his overseer told him that the prisoner got home Two hours by sun Monday morning."[44] Porter also noted that Daniel was home on the Monday of the rebellion. Both enslavers spoke to the character of the men they enslaved and to the fact that both enslaved men were located within the bounds of their enslaver's land during the rebellion.

Those who testified against people they enslaved provided the court with evidence that exposes the fraught emotions of surviving a slave rebellion. Jacob Williams remembered that before he went to measure timber on his land, he saw Nelson, whom he enslaved, and that "at the time a suspicion occurred to the witness that the prisoner [Nelson] had some intention of attacking him." Later that day, Jacob Williams returned home from his work to find his family murdered.[45] Mary Barrow remembered that Lucy, an enslaved woman, held her arm. She testified that "she [did] not know certainly what her intentions were but thought it was to detain her."[46] Were these enslavers, bereaved of spouses and family members, ambivalent about the enslaved people on trial? Did they extend the benefit of the doubt to the people they enslaved because acknowledging Black agency would acknowledge how fragile their mastery was? Were they worried about the level of compensation the state could offer them? Or did they feel that they should have a voice in the fate of their own human property? Whatever their motivation, they spoke up. So did other members of their community; other witnesses offered compelling evidence that led to guilty convictions.

The members of a white society that had built a legal system to serve their interests found limited success when their rights as individuals were considered against those of the commonwealth. The living enslavers of enslaved defendants met with defeat when they attempted to advocate for their human property. Virginia's legal structure benefited their class and the system within which they built wealth in human property. Enslaved defendants faced charges brought by the Commonwealth of Virginia, not by individual enslavers or other whites. Enslavers found their authority changed and challenged. The state would compensate them for their financial loss, but it would not excuse their inability to control enslaved people. Instead, the commonwealth would expect adherence to authority, even if in doing so enslavers lost valuable property.

Enslaved people held in custody in the local jail faced a shifting terrain with each rotation of the bench on each court date. As with long-established geographies of surveillance and control on individual farms, the geography of incarceration and punishment that consisted of the jailhouse, the court-house, the courtroom, and the hanging tree was changeable. Black voices from the extant trial record confirm that enslaved and free people built a competing geography of evasion and resistance even as whites increased their vigilance, violence, and repression.

Emerging Geographies of Evasion and Survival

On farms large and small, Black people's movement between sites of labor and residences facilitated a dynamic flow of information and experience. Their strategies for communicating valuable information did not disappear when militia captured and imprisoned Black people. Instead, African Americans formed new geographies of evasion and survival as they circulated through each site in downtown Jerusalem. Prisoners walked regularly between the courthouse and the jailhouse. Witnesses connected the court and the jail to the wider community. Those who were not themselves prisoners returned to Black communities.

The defendants held in the county jail were not the only African Americans who participated in the proceedings.[47] In all, free and enslaved African

Americans appeared by way of deposition in twenty-three of the fifty trials held at the court of oyer and terminer after the rebellion.[48] Of those twenty-three appearances, twelve were by African American women. Some appeared more than once. Six enslaved women, one enslaved girl, and one free woman of color appeared in total. Most appeared as part of the prosecution's case.[49] This was not particular to Black women; of the thirty-two times Black men appeared as witnesses, only eight appearances were on behalf of the defense.[50] The appearances of Black women at court give voice to their experiences during the rebellion, their participation in rebellion events, and their strategies for survival before, during, and after the rebellion.

It is hard to discern agency in the actions of enslaved witnesses who had no power to refuse white legal authorities because they feared for their own lives. The justices wielded real power over each defendant. And the sheriff wielded power over the African Americans they held in custody, some of whom became witnesses in each other's trials. When enslaved people entered the proceedings as witnesses, whites in various roles expected them to perform specific functions. But the depositions that are preserved in county minute books are valuable as a record of survival strategies.

On September 1, 1831, the second day of criminal proceedings related to the Southampton Rebellion, another enslaved person from Richard Porter's place provided key evidence in trials related to the rebellion. The voice of Venus, an enslaved woman, was heard, albeit indirectly, as the attorney for the commonwealth read her deposition aloud in the courtroom.

Looking at Venus and the other Black women who circulated between the courthouse, the jail, and the gallows allows a clearer view of how African Americans built a new geography of resistance as whites did their best to salvage and enforce their geography of control. With only one exception, enslaved and free women remained outside the county seat's geography of incarceration as suspects and defendants. They had mobility around downtown Jerusalem. Venus first appeared in chapter 2 as a purveyor of intelligence along the rebellion route. But we know of her role in the rebellion only because of her entrance and exit from the court as a holder of information that white men recognized as credible. The actions of Venus and women like her came from a will to survive in hostile terrain. While Venus's deposition conformed to the designs of the prosecutor who deposed her, what the county clerk saw fit to record of her words provides an outline of the geography of resistance and evasion that African Americans created and navigated in the days after the Southampton Rebellion.

At the bar were Jack and Andrew, two men enslaved by Catharine Whitehead, who had been killed in the rebellion. They were among the first rebels to be tried and sentenced. Their early trials reveal quite a bit about the court's priorities and motivations. The prosecutor for the commonwealth also established patterns in these early trials that point to his and the state's priorities. Just the day before, Tom, also enslaved by Whitehead, had stood trial and justices had acquitted him. Jack and Andrew would have known Tom and they would have known how his case ended. But unlike the available information about Tom's trial, Jack and Andrew's records include the testimony given by enslaved witnesses.

What happened at the Whitehead place exemplified the terror of the Southampton Rebellion for whites. There, rebels murdered an entire white household mostly made up of white women and girls. They murdered Catharine Whitehead, a widow and the owner of a successful farm. But on August 31 and September 1, when men from her farm stood trial, white authorities were not certain who had murdered Catharine Whitehead and her entire household, which consisted of her children, Richard, Margaret, Minerva, Mary Ann, and Mourning Ann, and her toddler grandson. Jack and Andrew were not accused of murdering Whitehead and her family.

Instead, Jack and Andrew faced a broader charge, that they had "consulted, advised and conspired with each other and with Divers other slaves to rebel and make insurrection and for making insurrection and taking the lives of divers free white persons of this Commonwealth."[51] It would have been hard for the court to ignore the brutality of the Whiteheads' murders. But being enslaved by Catharine Whitehead did not automatically denote guilt, as Tom's trial the day before had illustrated. The commonwealth used the testimony of two additional enslaved men from the Whitehead farm, Hubbard and Wallace, to account for Jack and Andrew's comings and goings during the rebellion. None of the evidence the prosecution brought tied the two men to a specific murder on Catharine Whitehead's farm or any other farm. Instead, the testimony of white and Black witnesses asserted that Jack and Andrew were not on the Whitehead place when the murders happened.

As their trials demonstrate, local authorities had trouble ascertaining who was a witness to and who had participated in the violence. The prosecution used Venus's account of Jack and Andrew's whereabouts to demonstrate that they had not stayed at the Whitehead place during the events of the rebellion. She confirmed that she met the two men, both on one horse, at the Porter place, where she lived. She admitted that she had told them that "the negroes had left word for them to go on after them" because they asked her for information about the rebels and their whereabouts. The prosecutor used Venus's recollection to establish that Jack and Andrew intended to join the rebellion, although on that point, her testimony included a hint of doubt. She remembered that "they did not know what else to do, and they went off" before she admitted that she assumed they had gone on to find the group of men in active rebellion.[52]

Venus likely knew the defendants. An enslaved man from the same farm where she was held in bondage was the first to be sentenced to death by the court. She knew that Richard Porter had spoken on Daniel's behalf at his trial. On a farm with thirty enslaved people, it was impossible that Venus did not know Daniel. The Porter place was near the Whitehead farm, where the defendants Jack and Andrew lived. Venus, Jack, and Andrew had probably crossed paths over the years in the neighborhood. Venus most likely also knew the state's other Black witnesses. Hubbard, who was also enslaved on the Whitehead place, testified to an interaction similar to the one Venus had with Jack and Andrew: they returned to the Whitehead place to ask if the rebels had come and gone. Wallace, who was also enslaved by Whitehead, remembered that the two men ran off as soon as insurgents arrived and that they were grieved and upset to learn of the murders on the Whitehead farm when they returned. He confirmed that they had visited two white men, Mr. Booth and Mr. Powell, before returning home. All three, Venus, Hubbard, and Wallace, were witnesses for the Commonwealth of Virginia; the prosecutor deposed them to support his cases against Jack and Andrew. All three confirmed that Jack and Andrew had left the Whitehead farm at one point or another during the rebellion. But all three also managed to cast doubt on what the two men had been doing during that time.

The defense countered with the testimonies of three free men, one Black and two white. Thomas Haithcock (sometimes spelled "Hathcock"), a free man of color, testified to Jack and Andrew's grief. Two white men, John (or possibly George) Booth and James Powell, testified to Jack and Andrew's deferent nature and their grief at the death of Catharine Whitehead, cor

roborating Wallace's testimony. Powell made clear that neither man had
fled when he called to them and that they had accompanied him to Cross
Keys, a safe haven for whites during the rebellion, without resisting. The
court clerk noted in his record that Jack "appeared to be much disturbed"
during his trial. Although the defense attorney built a case around Jack
and Andrew's demeanor and character, his witnesses still confirmed that
Jack and Andrew had spent time away from Catharine Whitehead's place
during the rebellion. None of them could speak about the contact, if any,
they had had with the band of rebels. Neither the prosecution nor the
defense could account for the whereabouts of Jack and Andrew when the
Whitehead murders took place.

In the cases of Jack and Andrew, the justices pronounced the defendants
guilty and sentenced the prisoners to hang. Then they formally recommended that the governor of Virginia "commute punishment of the prisoner." The justices would have seen this recommendation as merciful and
economical. Money from the sale of "criminal slaves" could help balance the
money the commonwealth spent compensating enslavers for the enslaved
laborers they had lost.[53]

The testimonies witnesses gave for the prosecution and the defense during the trials of Jack and Andrew map a route of their activities during the
rebellion. The two men fled the farm when the rebels arrived. They returned
to find that Catharine Whitehead and her family had been murdered. They
visited neighbors and eventually ended up at Cross Keys. The testimony in
their trial illuminates important networks in the community. The prosecutor used this narrative of their movement through their neighborhood to
win guilty convictions in both cases. Neither could be identified as murder-
ers or originators of the rebellion plot. But their movements and questions
about their activities rendered them too suspicious to allow for verdicts of
not guilty.

Venus was connected to the other witnesses, all of whom were residents
of her neighborhood. The court proceedings condensed the physical geography of their neighborhood first into the space of the courtroom and later,
by the clerk's hand, into the space of a few large minute book pages.[54] After
her testimony in the cases of Jack and Andrew, she went back to the Porter
place and rejoined the community of survivors beyond the geography of
downtown Jerusalem.

Although enslaved witnesses like Venus, Hubbard, and Wallace did not have a choice about whether to cooperate with the court, they still had some agency. One limitation of the trials is revealed in what those witnesses did not offer the court: none of them offered information beyond the limited testimonies asked of them. Together, their testimonies cast doubt about whether each defendant was guilty. None provided definitive answers about what Jack and Andrew were up to during the entirety of the rebellion. Venus, specifically, admitted to having advanced knowledge that Hubbard and Wallace did not or would not admit to when questioned. Of the three, Venus most deftly walked a thin line: she told Jack and Andrew where to go but did not tell them information that was specific enough to land her in jail.[55]

The court found the defendants guilty in each case that enslaved Black women gave testimonies for. Except for the cases of Jack and Andrew, none came with a recommendation from the justices that the governor commute the sentences to transfer from Virginia. The involvement of enslaved women in court proceedings did not inspire leniency and their words, even those that cast doubt on each defendant's guilt, did not dissuade the court from sentencing defendants to execution.

But their testimonies offer a window into enslaved women's experiences of the rebellion and their ability to evade suspicion of their own involvement. Two enslaved women, Delsey and Mary, gave testimony in the trial of Moses, an enslaved man, on the same day as Venus in early September. Under duress, at the center of white male power, these women's words circulated through the court, one to defend her neighbor and the other to provide testimony against him. As was the case with Venus's statement, their testimonies concerned proximity and mobility.

Moses, who was enslaved by John T. Barrow, stood trial for his involvement in the rebellion on September 1, 1831, right after the trials of Jack and Andrew concluded. John T. Barrow met his death during the rebellion as he attempted to defend his home and give his wife, Mary, time to escape. But Moses's trial did not bring to light any information about his enslaver's death. Instead, five of six witnesses in the case placed Moses at Dr. Samuel Blunt's house during the rebellion. The Blunt farm was northeast of but not next to the Barrow place. Most people present in the courtroom that day would have known this and understood that Moses was far away from

Barrow's control as the rebellion moved through the neighborhood. Those present would also have known that the rebels attacked the Blunt place. The prosecution brought evidence from a group of witnesses who swore that Moses was actively involved in the rebellion at the Blunt place, that he chased down an enslaved woman and a young white girl in the Blunt garden, and that he willingly joined the rebel band.

Mary, a woman enslaved by the Blunts, was an important witness for the prosecution. Witnesses said that Moses chased Mary down outside the Blunt home. Mary confirmed that she ran into the garden. But like Venus had in the cases previous, Mary cast subtle doubt on Moses's guilt. She did not make clear if Moses pursued her or if she saw him cause harm to any white women. Instead, she testified that "her Mistress Mrs. Blunt told her to take her child and make her escape with her, that she ran down in the garden," then she "became so fatigued and frightened that she put the child down and told her to get in the bushes."[56] According to Mary's testimony, she then returned to the Blunt house, where she met an enslaved man wearing a "light colored cap."[57] This detail of clothing was used to identify Moses when testimony presented by the prosecutor corroborated it.

While Mary gave testimony for the prosecution, the details of her story provide a blueprint of evasion and survival. Her sworn statement appears in the court record because it helped the prosecution identify Moses as one of the men present at the Blunt place during the rebellion. But her testimony introduced doubt about the actions of members of her community at every opportunity. She never positively identified Moses as an assailant. She stated that it was Mrs. Blunt, not Moses's pursuit, that inspired her to flee into the garden. Even Mary's story of following Mrs. Blunt's instructions is revealing. She ran to the garden, a site of domestic labor she was familiar with. And then she left the Blunts' daughter to hide there and fend for herself while she doubled back and met an enslaved man associated with the rebellion. She noted that although she was tired and afraid as she ran away from the rebels, she chose to leave her white charge and head back toward them, implying that running to rebels was less frightening than attempting to escape them. In the space of very brief testimony, she served the needs of the prosecution and demonstrated how she used a site of labor, the Blunt garden, to evade suspicion (by helping a white child) and to evade violent reprisals from male rebels (by returning to them). Her testimony enabled her to evade being charged with conspiring to rebel. She was, as she claimed, simply following a white woman's instructions while remaining within the bounds of the Blunt farm.

This was not the only way an enslaved woman demonstrated how to survive the rebellion. Delsey, who was enslaved by Rebecca Vaughn, provided testimony for Moses's defense. Her importance to the trial is best understood through community dynamics and the physical geography in the neighborhood where the rebellion took place. First, whites in the courtroom that day had particular kinship and community ties. Moses's deceased enslaver, John T. Barrow, was connected to one justice who presided over Moses's case: James W. Parker was Barrow's brother-in-law, the husband of his wife's sister. Parker's wife and Barrow's wife had grown up with Moses on their family's place. Moses had been a part of a property transfer that was common between whites in the community who used enslaved people to bolster the economic prospects of their offspring. Mrs. Parker and Mrs. Barrow were both daughters of Rebecca Vaughn. Mrs. Vaughn, whom rebels murdered, owned the farm where Moses had spent a significant portion of his life. Second, justices would have had knowledge of the location of the Barrow, Vaughn, and Blunt farms. While the Barrow farm and the Vaughn place were along the same road, the rebels' path through the neighborhood allegedly brought Moses far northeast of the Barrow place (see map 3). Delsey's testimony hinged on the court's understanding of these white kinship connections, a long-ago transfer of human property, and the plausibility of the journey from farm to farm that her testimony confirmed.[58]

Delsey stated that Moses was at the Vaughn place during the rebellion, confirming the testimony of one of the witnesses for the prosecution. Frank, an enslaved man who lived on the Blunt farm, had already testified for the prosecution that rebels had coerced Moses into joining them. He also stated that Moses was present on the Blunt place only because a white neighbor, Newt Drew, had told him to go to the Vaughn farm. If Drew had not instructed Moses to head to the Vaughn farm to "see what the news was," Moses would not have crossed paths with the band of rebels and they would not have forced him to join them. Frank explained that when he was captured, Moses said that he had been forced to join and that he had only ventured out because Newt Drew had asked him to. To substantiate this, the defense needed to confirm that Moses had followed directions from

Drew and gone to the Vaughn place. Rebels had stopped at the Vaughn place just before going to the Blunts' home to the northeast and would have met Moses along the way.[59] Delsey, who was enslaved on the Vaughn place and was familiar with Moses, was perfectly positioned to attest to Moses's whereabouts, the fact that the rebels had recruited him, and his actions that day.

She testified that Moses had been at the Vaughn farm the evening before the attack at the Blunts' place. He had not been present when rebels attacked his enslaver's farm. It was completely plausible that Moses, who had been enslaved by the Vaughns before his move to the Barrow place in 1828, might have any number of reasons to visit the Vaughn place. The next morning, he met Newt Drew on the road and Drew ordered him home. According to Delsey, a group of insurgents attacked the Vaughn place the next morning about 45 minutes after Moses came back. At that point, the rebellion had already come and gone at the Barrow place, where Moses lived. Given his timing, Moses missed the attack at the Barrow farm, met Newt Drew along the road, and arrived back at the Vaughn place shortly thereafter. Delsey testified that "the insurgents were seen coming about three hundred yards off . . . [and] that they required the prisoner to go with them[,] which he objected to." She added that "they threatened him [and] gave him arms and he went off with them."[60] Delsey confirmed that rebels forced Moses to join them, which explained his appearance at the Blunt farm north of the Vaughn place on the second day of the rebellion. Her testimony was compelling because of her rootedness to the Vaughn farm, her knowledge of the same family and kinship connections that whites in the courtroom understood, and the court's understanding of the geography of the neighborhood.

The court would also have known about the Vaughn place and the murder of Rebecca Vaughn and her children, Ann Eliza and Arthur. Delsey may have been the "venerable negro woman" who "described the scene which she had witnessed" of the murder of the Vaughn family "with great emphasis" to the *Constitutional Whig*, a Richmond paper. The paper published the news of the rebellion on the day of Moses's trial.[61] This unnamed "old negress . . . described the horrors of the scene," the paper recorded, "in a most lively and picturesque manner."[62] But this newspaper account, like Delsey's testimony, included no details about who exactly had attacked the Vaughn place or who had recruited Moses as he waited on horseback in the Vaughn yard. Delsey admitted under questioning that Moses "could have escaped while the insurgents were coming up."[63] But beyond this line in her brief appearance in the trial record, Delsey remained short on details.

The defense also used testimony from Hark, who was enslaved by Joseph Travis. Later Hark would be revealed to be an original co-conspirator in Nat Turner's confession. But at the time, authorities had jailed Hark as one of many enslaved men held on suspicion of participation in the rebellion. First, Hark confirmed that Moses had joined the insurgents during the rebellion and that he had "joined them voluntarily—that they were together some time[,] that he was in the company that went to Dr. Blunts." The defense must have hoped the court would pay more attention to Hark's final bit of testimony, his statement "that the witness did not get to the house, but the prisoner went on and he saw no more of him."[64] According to Hark, Moses went along with rebels but did not participate in any murders and disappeared while the group focused on attacking the Blunt place. Combined with Delsey's testimony, the defense made the case that while Moses had been swept up in the rebellion under duress, he ultimately ducked out and did not participate in killings.

After these testimonies, Newt Drew's version of events entered the record. In contrast to Moses's story, Drew denied ordering Moses to visit the Vaughn place. Instead, Drew stated that he "ordered him to go home."[65] Of course, given Moses's history, it is reasonable to wonder if home for him was the Vaughn farm. Neither the court nor Moses's defense attorney pursued that question. Instead, Drew had the final word of testimony in Moses's case. The court pronounced Moses guilty. They sentenced him to hang and valued him at $400. And then, after a long day of trials, they prepared to adjourn.[66]

Two days later on September 3, 1831, the testimony of Cynthia, who was enslaved by Jacob Williams, was read in the case of Nelson, a man whom Williams also enslaved. The record does not specify if she testified for the commonwealth or in Nelson's defense. Her testimony could be perceived as both damaging and helpful to his case. Testimony against Nelson from both Jacob Williams and his overseer, Caswell Worrell, placed Nelson on the farm and even in the fields on the morning of the rebellion. While the overseer remembered a vague warning from Nelson the week before, neither white man took Nelson's odd behavior or illness on the morning of the rebellion seriously. However, in hindsight both men were certain of his guilt.[67]

Cynthia's vantage point in the Williamses' kitchen provided information that neither white man could. Jacob Williams left the farm to measure timber and Caswell Worrell escaped before rebels could overtake him. Neither were present when rebels arrived and began murdering the members of the Williams family who were in the house. Williams's wife, Nancy, and their three children, all of whom were under the age of four, did not escape.[68] From the kitchen, Cynthia noticed that Nelson came in from the fields early and changed his clothes. Shortly after Nelson had returned, rebels rode onto the Williams place. She told the court that when she saw Nelson he was in his best clothing. He met her in the kitchen after the murders "while the negroes were in the yard" and he asked for and then took "his Mistresses meat out of the pot [and] cut a piece off" while she stood there.[69] Hauntingly, her last memory of Nelson was his parting words: "Cynthia you do not know me." He added, "I do not know when you will see me again." Tacked on to her recorded testimony, perhaps in answer to a lawyer's probing question, she admitted that when Nelson left, he "stepped over the dead bodies without any manifestation of grief."[70]

Cynthia was silent about what else she saw in the kitchen that morning. If not for that last sentence in the record, the timeline of events and her position on the Williams place might have remained murky. But the bodies, the remains of Mrs. Williams and her children, substantiate Nelson's timeline. He didn't arrive in the kitchen until *after* the murders. Of course, for her to know that, she needed to have been present in the kitchen. She did not speak about how she continued working in a kitchen with multiple bodies nearby.[71] She did not say where she was when the murders occurred or even who specifically committed them. She made only this one appearance in the court record and did not say that Nelson had any involvement with the murders. As Delsey and Venus had done, Cynthia gave testimony that had many gaps and silences. The words she did speak cast doubt about the guilt of Black men. Cynthia testified and remained beyond white suspicion.

The Trial of Lucy

The next enslaved woman entered the court record on September 19, 1831. By that time, Black men had been executed on three days. On September 5, 9, and 12, the local sheriff had carried out twelve hangings. Twelve men of prime fieldhand age had been hanged for all to see at a time when an important harvest was approaching. The violence had not ended there. At some point during these early weeks of trials and executions, Nat Turner's wife was publicly beaten. As a result of the beating, she surrendered some of his papers that were described as "filled with hieroglyphical characters, conveying no definite meaning." There was also "a piece of paper, of a late date, which, all agree, is a list of his men; if so, they were short of [had fewer than] twenty."[72] Whether his force numbered in the hundreds or fewer than twenty, Nat Turner remained at large. Justices had tried men who were key lieutenants in the insurgency like Sam, Hark, and Dred, and their trials had yielded no real testimony about who specifically had committed murders at each of the rebels' stops. Time and again, witnesses, even those for the commonwealth, claimed that defendants had gone reluctantly with the band of rebels. Perhaps it was the thin nature of the evidence that led to more commuted sentences and acquittals as justices realized the volume of cases they had to handle. Executions came with fees for the jailer and the sheriff and bills for the commonwealth, which was obliged by law to compensate enslavers for enslaved people who were found guilty of capital crimes. But Lucy, who was enslaved by John T. Barrow, was not another witness; she was a defendant charged with conspiring to rebel.

The case against Lucy hinged on two key factors: her proximity to and close relationships with known rebels and her actions during the rebellion. During her trial, Lucy's enslaver, Mary T. Barrow, testified that Lucy had held her as rebels approached her farm. Mrs. Barrow's husband, John T. Barrow, had done his best to fend off rebels at the couple's front door while she made her escape out the back. However, Lucy, who had positioned herself behind the house so she could meet her, reached out and grabbed Mrs. Barrow's arm. After a brief tug-of-war between Lucy and another unnamed enslaved person, Mrs. Barrow was able to escape into the swamp. Mrs. Barrow was not sure that Lucy intended her harm in that moment. But had she remained in the yard, she certainly would have been murdered like her husband.

The enslaved person who helped Mary Barrow may have been Bird, the next witness in Lucy's case. However, Bird did not speak about the incident behind the Barrow house. Instead, he noted that Lucy and Moses, the same Moses Delsey had testified in defense of, shared a room where the militia had discovered a cache of stolen money. Like Moses, Lucy had been transferred by Rebecca Vaughn to her new son-in-law, John T. Barrow, in 1828. The court would have known of this white kinship connection when they tried Lucy. And they would have remembered the trial and conviction of Moses. Her connection to Moses, who had already been hanged by the time of her trial, would have stood out as another important community connection.[73]

A different Moses, probably the boy enslaved by the Joseph Travis who testified frequently throughout the trial, noted that Lucy conversed with rebels after the attacks were over on the Barrow farm. Her proximity to and communication with rebels bolstered the case of the prosecution. Yet every other enslaved woman who gave testimony in trials spoke with rebels during the rebellion. Venus passed information to Jack and Andrew. Delsey spoke with Moses in her front yard. Cynthia stood in the kitchen near where rebels had murdered her enslaver and did not stop Nelson from eating meat from her pot before he walked away, stepping over dead bodies as he went. In her own words, Lucy was innocent. And Robert T. Musgrave, who heard her confession, testified that she claimed to have hidden in the Barrow cornfields during the attacks. But the justices were unimpressed with Lucy's confession to Musgrave. Perhaps, when faced with Mrs. Barrow's testimony, they decided to defer to the widow's version of events. They pronounced Lucy guilty, sentenced her to hang on September 26, and valued her at $375.

Physical proximity to known and suspected rebels featured in the testimony of each enslaved woman. On September 22, Beck (or Becky), an enslaved girl, testified for the commonwealth in the trials of Jim and Issac. The two men were from Sussex County, which neighbored Southampton to the west. She also gave testimony in the trial of Frank, who was enslaved by Solomon Parker. She had gone almost unnoticed at a gathering on Solomon Parker's farm because of her young age. There, she had overheard grownups speaking about rebellion and insurrection; she identified Jim, Isaac, and Frank as present.[74] Charlotte and Cherry also gave testimony in the trial of Ben, the last enslaved man to be tried for participation in the rebellion on November 21, 1831. Both women lived on farms where rebels visited: Charlotte on Peter Edwards's place and Cherry on Salathiel Francis's farm. Both mentioned meeting with other insurgents during the rebellion.[75]

Each woman's testimony substantiated accusations that a defendant was close to known rebels and to the rebellion event. And each revealed their own closeness to those same events and same rebels, their neighbors and kin. Women were embedded in the geographies of the farms rebels visited.

No male participant could have denied the presence of Black women, and, as these women's brief appearances demonstrate, rebels spoke with them, learned important information from them, and even gave information to them. None of these women testified that a defendant in question committed a murder during the rebellion. With the exception of Lucy, who hanged for reaching out to hold her enslaver's wife, all of the women endured court proceedings and returned to their farms to live among the empty spaces left by those who had been murdered and those who had been executed. The same networks that became visible amid violent and legal reprisals after the rebellion continued to function beyond the geography of incarceration and punishment in downtown Jerusalem.

Free People on Trial

Free people of color had much to lose in the wake of the rebellion. From the fall of 1831 through 1832, leaders in Richmond considered what they should do with Virginia's significant free Black population. The rebellion exacerbated white people's fears of that group. While state politicians wrestled with the question of how to respond to the rebellion in a way that preserved racial hierarchy and profitable labor regimes, the white response to the rebellion was local.[76]

During the rebellion, the militia apprehended and took into custody a small group of free men of color and one free youth. The sheriff held them in jail to be interviewed by local justices, even though those justices could not try free people of color for capital crimes in local criminal courts.[77] Instead, the justices' role was limited to determining if four free men and one youth should be tried. In cases where justices charged a person who was not enslaved "with any treason, murder, felony, or other crime or offence whatsoever against this commonwealth,"[78] it was up to those justices to determine if the case should be referred to the higher court or if the accused could be tried in a local criminal court. The commonwealth considered the participation of free people of color in slave rebellion and insurrection to be a capital offense.[79] According to Virginia law, local justices were required "to hold a court of *examination*; which court, consisting of five members, at least, shall consider whether the prisoner may be discharged from further prosecution, or may be tried in the county, or in the district (now circuit) court."[80] Unlike the criminal trials held for enslaved people, the court records for free Black people note only when these examinations occurred and if justices remanded them to jail or released them from custody.

It is difficult to know what information justices received from free Black people beyond what free Black witnesses provided in the trials of enslaved people. Only two free people of color appear by name as witnesses in the trials that took place in the fall of 1831: Eliza Crathenton, who appeared in chapter 3, and Thomas Haithcock. Haithcock was himself interviewed by local justices and held in jail throughout the trials. He would not stand trial and face judgment until the following spring. Eliza Crathenton, like the seven enslaved women deposed during the trials, appeared in court to speak about people she knew. Just like women before and after her, she served as a link between the geography of incarceration in downtown Jerusalem and the nearby neighborhoods most affected by the rebellion.

Issues for Free Black People in the Aftermath of the Rebellion

On September 7, 1831, Hardy, a man enslaved by Benjamin Edwards, faced the panel of justices. His was the twenty-second trial the court heard. Three enslaved men provided testimony. Hark gave evidence in Hardy's defense. Henry and Harry gave evidence for the prosecution. None could account for Hardy's whereabouts on August 22 but all three could confirm that Hardy had been in the presence of Black men who favored the rebels. Henry gave the most detailed account. He testified that Hardy was enthusiastic when he delivered the incorrect news that "the English were in the County killing white people." Henry remembered that Hardy responded that "it was nothing and ought to have been done long ago—that the negroes had been punished long enough."[81]

Eliza Crathenton's words depart from this narrative. Her memory of events paint Hardy as conflicted. Crathenton received the same information as the male witnesses: Hardy intended to join Nat Turner. But her response was different, as was her impression of Hardy's commitment to the rebellion. The record states that "Eliza Crathenton[,] a free woman being charged and sworn as a witness for the prisoner[,] says the prisoner and two others told her they meant to join Genl. Nat. and she dissuaded them from it."[82] The record does not make clear when this interaction took place. But it does state that Crathenton believed she'd convinced Hardy not to take part in the rebellion. She was sure enough to appear in court.[83]

Unlike the men who appeared before the justices to speak about Hardy's behavior, Eliza Crathenton appeared to speak about her own actions. She did not testify that she tried to dissuade Hardy or that she warned him. She testified that "she dissuaded" him.[84] The court could dwell on the plot of the still-truant Nat Turner if they wanted to, but Eliza Crathenton had them know that her instructions were heeded, and not "General Nat's." It was a bold claim. And she was confident enough to lend her testimony to Hardy's defense.[85]

Thomas Haithcock's name appears throughout court documents as a free man of color who supported the Southampton Rebellion. Haithcock appeared in court proceedings as a witness, in the testimony of other witnesses, and as a suspected rebel. Various witnesses of the events of the rebellion placed him in circulation around the neighborhood. He appeared as a witness in the trials of Jack and Andrew on September 1, where he spoke about how they grieved for their enslaver.[86] In Hardy's trial, two witnesses noted in their testimony for the prosecution that Thomas Haithcock came to the Edwards place with four boys in tow to recruit Hardy.[87] He appeared in testimony against Ben on November 21, during the final trial before justices. A witness placed Thomas Haithcock and Billy Artis, also a free man, with Ben at the Francis place, the site of a number of murders.[88] Unlike Eliza Crathenton, he moved throughout the neighborhood. Also unlike her, he actively recruited while she actively dissuaded potential participants in the rebellion.

Both Eliza Crathenton and Thomas Haithcock demonstrate how free people of color participated in Black resistive networks. Their participation was heavily dictated by gender and opposing assessments of the possibility for the rebellion to succeed. Thomas Haithcock moved between farms to recruit for the rebellion. Eliza Crathenton, like other women in the neighborhood, stayed put but exercised influence from her own vantage point. Both Eliza Crathenton and Thomas Haithcock became hubs of information and authority during rebellion. The court proceedings demonstrate that their positions in the community were legible to white authorities in the courtroom. Attorneys believed them enough to ask for their testimony and justices accepted, at least tacitly, their positions of influence among free and enslaved Black people.

The record does not make clear why Eliza Crathenton chose to discourage men from participating in the rebellion. But we do know that she believed that Hardy had listened to her. The record of Thomas Haithcock's trial, which took place in the spring of 1832, provides evidence of how the women in his life responded to his enthusiastic involvement in the rebellion. His daughter testified that both she and his wife pleaded with him to stay clear of the rebellion and its leader. They echoed Crathenton's stance when each assessed the situation and judged that their survival was best served by watching and waiting.[89] Free women, at least this small group of them, were in agreement: the rebellion was not the right path to choose. And they were not wrong. The rebellion destabilized Black communities and inspired whites to further challenge the free Black community's already tenuous freedom.

Free People of Color in the Courtroom

The Southampton Rebellion and the suspected involvement of multiple free men of color led to white scrutiny of free Black people in the commonwealth. It was not the first or last time that white Virginians got antsy about the free Black people who lived in the commonwealth.[90] Free people of color who escaped the initial violence of the rebellion and remained out of custody took every opportunity authorities afforded them to assert their free status. One way they did so was registering themselves as free people with the county. They did so between the trials of suspected rebels, court business that directed executions, and interviews of alleged free Black participants in the rebellion. Amid proceedings in the center of a geography meant to demonstrate the powerlessness of African Americans, free people arrived to make their freedom known.

Virginia law required free people of color to register with their local municipality every year.[91] Free African Americans appeared at county court dates throughout 1831 to register as free persons, just as they had for decades. A sample of a registry of free people of color has survived. More registries are embedded in the county's court minute books, many of which have survived.[92] Registries appear in the county court minute book for March, April, and June of 1831. Accounting for the free population of the county was a mundane task for local magistrates. For free people of color, registry entailed a fee and the dangers of making oneself conspicuous. As previously discussed, free status remained tenuous because of cycles of poverty and debt that often resulted in the common need to live on white-owned land to secure employment. But registry also offered free people a way to prove their free status. Their status as free people did not denote equality with whites and it did not guarantee them the right to remain in Southampton County.[93] But it did afford free Black people the opportunity to assert belonging and freedom at a tumultuous moment in the county's history.[94]

On October 17, 1831, a small group of free people of color, called "free negroes" in court records, arrived to register as free. By then local justices had spent fifteen court dates dealing with forty-two trials and interviews, among other pieces of court business.[95] The record of October 17 includes only two trials related to the rebellion. Nearly five pages of the court minute book detail the regular business of the court that day. The sheriff, Clement Rochelle, whom the court had called upon to recruit guards for the jailhouse, needed to compile a list of citizens who were delinquent in paying their land taxes. He also needed to be paid by the county for his service over the previous two months.[96] Justices handled the cases of three enslaved men that day. But before that, the justices saw to court business that occupied three pages in the minute book, including the "registers of Jervis Ricks, Edney Ricks & Silky Diggs," which the court ordered "to be certified as Freely made."[97] They were the first free Black people to register since the rebellion.[98]

Two pages later, a substantial group of free people appear in the record. The clerk recorded the registrations of Zelpha Jones, Silas Scott, Mary Diggs, Hannah Basrone (possibly Brown), Milly Whitfield, Betsy Whitfield, Fortune Scott, Penny Copeland, Isham Whitfield, Sally Whitfield, Sofehia (possibly Sophia) Jones, Dolly Butcher, Miles Roberts, Anthony Browne, and Milly Browne as free people.[99] The next page recorded the court's judgment in two cases that involved a total of three men. Jack and Shadrach, both enslaved by Nathaniel Simmons, had been charged with treason. The court decided that it could not try enslaved people for treason and discharged the two men from custody. Sam, who was enslaved by Peter Edwards, was not so lucky. Two white men and one enslaved man testified against him. His enslaver spoke on his behalf. The court issued a guilty verdict and sentenced Sam to hang.[100] All of this happened as free people of color circulated through the courthouse and back out into the county.

The next day, October 18, 1831, the court was back in session. In between court proceedings, free people of color again arrived to register with local officials. That day, a free woman named Pleasant Cotton came to the courthouse. But unlike the eighteen people the day before, she came to make sure her previously made registration was in order. The clerk noted that she required a new certificate because her "former certificate has been mislaid or lost."[101] Then the court moved on to try Archer, a man enslaved by Arthur B. Reece. They then interviewed Isham Turner, a free man of color. Justices decided to remand him to jail, then they attended to the registration of Frank Vines, Eley Vines, and Paul Vines. They tried Moses, an enslaved boy who gave important testimony in other key cases. The court ruled him guilty and recommended that the governor allow him to be sold from the state.

Then the court ordered that payments be made and saw to estates. They ended the day by registering Matilda Ricks, Fanny Ricks, Rebecca Butler, and Dolly Butler.[102] The surnames of registrants suggest possible family and kinship connections. These free people of color would have traveled together to Jerusalem through the hostile landscape of post-rebellion Southampton County to register. They circulated through the courthouse and courtroom, past the hanging tree, and back to their home neighborhoods. Some would continue to work alongside enslaved people. Others would return to their own land. All would hope that rootedness to the county and official registries would be enough to keep them together.

At the end of November and December 1831, after the trials related to the rebellion had ended, more free people appeared and registered.[103] Free people of color faced uncertainty at the close of 1831. They knew that after Nat Turner's death that November, whites would want to return to the status quo. They could not be sure, though, that they would be included in the return to old hierarchies that whites so desperately wanted. One way to subvert white efforts to expel them was to assert free status and residency. Many of the surnames that appear have roots in local registries that date back to the beginning of the nineteenth century.[104] Some of those same surnames belonged to prominent whites who, in an attempt to live the promise of the American Revolution or as the result of religious conviction, had manumitted the people they enslaved. The free people of color who arrived to register belonged to a liminal class of free persons who were not strangers to whites. They were long-standing fixtures in the county and on the white-owned farms that dotted it. Appearing and registering was one way to reassert deep roots in a county that some rightly feared might be poised to expel them.

Bound for Survival: Indenture Contracts as Strategies of Resistance

Some free people took drastic steps to ensure they would remain with their families. For some, this meant leaving Southampton County for other states or, more famously, as part of the efforts of the Colonization Society of Virginia to remove free Black people to West Africa. Others decided to remain in the county they considered home. In addition to records of registry, indentures or apprenticeship contract proceedings also appeared in the minute books of fall 1831 in Southampton County. Binding free Black children as apprentices to white masters was not uncommon in antebellum Virginia. As previously discussed, the overseers of the poor frequently bound both white and free Black children to heads of what they deemed to be stable households when those children were destitute or orphaned. Apprenticeships that concerned eight children in four families occurred during and directly after court proceedings related to the Southampton Rebellion. These records, tucked in amid the records of trials, suggest that binding out children was another survival strategy for free Black families. Binding free Black children to white masters tied them to local farms.

After the rebellion, the apprenticeship system provided an avenue for stability in a changed geography of surveillance and control. It most commonly served as a social welfare practice throughout the United States. The system had an exploitative side: at times overseers of the poor removed children from Black parents and forced them into as many as eighteen to twenty-one years of labor. All over the country, authorities used the practice of apprenticeship as a means of social control. Standards of fitness often required things that many of the nation's poor simply could not meet. Those who agreed to become the master of apprenticed children balanced the cost of maintaining them with the labor they provided during their term of service. This labor made destitute children attractive charges for prospective masters and, at least according to apprentice law, provided children and young adults with the skills they needed to become self-supporting adults.[105]

Parents sometimes appeared in court to bind their children out voluntarily. A variety of circumstances influenced this decision. Some parents
chose apprenticeship with tradesmen as their child's best chance at survival
or upward mobility. But for free Black parents navigating the unstable social
terrain of post-rebellion Southampton County, their decision to bind out
their children was born of racial inequality, poverty, and a legal system that
at times required ties to white citizens for stability.

Black parents' concerns about social stability were well founded in the
fall of 1831. Virginia whites had shown interest in colonization in West
Africa as a way to rid the commonwealth of its free Black population in the
previous decade. Legislators had already attempted to restrict the ability
of manumitted individuals to remain in the commonwealth.[106] That fall,
powerful legislators in Richmond began debating what to do about public
safety, slavery, and free people of color after the rebellion inflamed white
fears. In early December 1831, Governor John Floyd delivered a speech that
pointed to free Black people as instigators and argued that the commonwealth needed harsher laws to curb their potentially dangerous influence
on enslaved people.[107] While free Black people ultimately did not experience
large-scale removal from the commonwealth in the years after the rebellion,
in the fall of 1831, free Black parents had no way of knowing the outcome of
new legislation and how local officials would act. With this post-rebellion
uncertainty, free adults, the majority of whom lived as a part of white
households, may have seen binding their children to white masters as a
way to make sure their children remained in Southampton County and of
ensuring that their children would be cared for.[108]

At the end of September 1831, the overseers of the poor bound out Boyd
Whitfield, the son of Catharine Whitfield. Boyd had just turned 10 that August. Later, on November 21, 1831, one day after the last trial for a suspected
rebel, David and Diddy Byrd arrived in court to bind their children out to
a local white man named Benjamin Whitfield. David Byrd was a tailor, a
skilled laborer capable of supporting his wife and their five children.[109] No
court order forced the Byrds to apprentice their children, who were aged
5 through 13, and no order forced Catharine Whitfield to bind out her son
Boyd. But the Byrds decided that Diddy, Nancy, Henry, Anne, and Jane
Byrd would live with Benjamin Whitfield, their new master, until each girl
turned 18 and their son Henry turned 21.[110] Boyd Whitfield's new master,

William W. Cutler, also agreed to keep him until he turned 21. This ensured that each child would be tied to the county for at least five more years.

Neither Benjamin Whitfield nor William W. Cutler were typical white landowners in the county. Both lived on the south side of the Nottoway River in St. Luke's Parish, the part of the county where the Southampton Rebellion erupted. Both headed households: Whitfield a household of thirty-six and Cutler a household of twenty-eight. These numbers are typical, but the demographics of their households were not. Benjamin Whitfield's household included twenty-seven free people of color who ranged in age from children to adults.[111] Cutler's place was home to thirteen free people of color. Although both men had at one time enslaved very small numbers of people, neither held human property in 1830, the year before the rebellion.[112]

Whitfield's use of free Black labor may have been the result of his family history. In the late eighteenth century, another Benjamin Whitfield freed those he enslaved in his will. Although his descendants fought the will by petitioning local courts, the Free Negro Registry for Southampton County in the period 1800 to 1806 includes fourteen free people of color who listed Benjamin Whitfield as their former enslaver.[113] The surname Whitfield remained prominent in the free Black community. For example, the group of registrants in Southampton County's courtroom on October 17, 1831, included four Whitfields. The name Benjamin Whitfield appears for generations in Southampton County records for both white and Black county residents. The Benjamin Whitfield who became the master of David and Diddy Byrd's children in 1831 was most likely a grandson of the Benjamin Whitfield who manumitted the people he enslaved and the son of Reuben Whitfield, who fought his father's will. The Whitfield surname connects both apprenticeship proceedings. Catharine Whitfield may have descended from free people who were originally emancipated as a part of the Whitfield estate. Perhaps her connection to other Whitfields was how Catharine Whitfield knew about the apprentice system when, facing the uncertainty of the fall of 1831, she found a place for her son with a white landowner who could ensure that he would stay in Southampton County as part of a community of free people of color.

Not all children who were bound out had parents who participated in decisions about their apprenticeships. Early in 1832, while all five free people of color suspected of participation in the Southampton Rebellion remained in jail, the overseers of the poor bound another free Black child to a white man who was not an enslaver. In response to a court order in the fall of 1831, local officials bound John Artis, "of the age of five years ten months 11 days," to Samuel Story on January 16, 1832.[114] Story's household included only two whites and fifteen free people of color. Another Story, Zacheus, entered the record on February 14, 1832, as the new master of two free Black boys. Jack E. Turner, aged 8, and Josiah Turner, aged 6, would have company on their new master's farm; Zacheus Story already had three free boys under the age of 10 on his place. Zacheus could have chosen to apprentice young Black people rather than purchasing enslaved people for a number of reasons. It is possible that the prospect of raising cheap laborers who cost only their upkeep and a small sum of cash at the end of their contract made more financial sense to him than investing in enslaved labor. Zacheus Story enslaved two people, one a boy under 10 and the other a man of prime working age.[115] Officials listed no parents in formal paperwork for John Artis, Jack Turner, and Josiah Turner. They may have been taken from their parents or they may have been orphans. But they joined farms with established free Black populations.

Free Black people remained uncertain of their ability to stay in Virginia immediately after the rebellion. Even as trials moved forward in the local courthouse and free people of color awaited prosecution at the next meeting of the superior court in Southampton, white people were calling for the expulsion of free Black people from Virginia. While previous incarnations of the American Colonization Society and the colonization movement in Virginia had evangelical roots and had focused on manumission, whites who reignited the campaign to remove free people of color to Liberia after the rebellion cared about ridding the commonwealth of the danger they believed the free Black population posed. As Charles F. Irons notes in his study of Black and white Virginia evangelicals, "The Southampton and Norfolk branches of the Colonization Society of Virginia were the prime movers in this effort; they hastily gathered up approximately 350 Southampton County Black people, mostly free persons who survived the post-Turner reprisals, and sent them to Liberia in December 1831." Irons characterizes this as removal and as "more deportations than deeds of cooperative benevolence."[116] While colonization did not balloon into large-scale removal throughout the commonwealth and some free people certainly wanted to escape Virginia, this local response that was akin to removal would have been more important to free Black people in Southampton County than debates in Richmond.

The Byrd and Whitfield children entered into labor contracts that would guarantee them a place in a free Black community. Perhaps both Whitfield and Cutler were sympathetic to the plight of free Black people. Some of the free people of color who emigrated to Liberia that winter had the surname Whitfield and may have been residing on Benjamin Whitfield's farm. By 1840, Benjamin Whitfield's household included only thirteen free people of color.[117] But no matter how each new white master treated the free children in their households, apprenticeships would keep them in Southampton County as part of the broader community of free and enslaved Black people.

In a season of death and mourning, enslaved people appeared at the courthouse and spoke. Some provided testimony that directly incriminated other enslaved people. But many more provided information that did not indicate that those they testified for and against had direct involvement in murders or the rebellion plot. None of Nat Turner's lieutenants were tried as key co-conspirators. Until Turner's confession was heard, the court had no clear narrative of how the rebellion was planned. Even though months of trials had demonstrated the many ways the African American community was involved, Turner took sole responsibility for the rebellion. He mentioned no one who had not been tried or executed and betrayed no local networks of support for the rebellion.

Free people of color appeared at the courthouse to register as free and continued to do so during the trials. Some bound out their children. Some later fled or were forced to flee the county for West Africa in search of freedom their home could not provide. All faced the uncertainty of harsher laws and wary whites. Indenture, apprenticeship, and labor that was contracted season to season may have guaranteed that they could live in the county, but exploitation and the brutal ways whites managed their labor forces was part of each system. Some free Black people stayed on in Southampton, no matter how bleak their prospects, in order to keep all of the members of their families, enslaved and free, together as much as was possible.

The business of survival moved forward for Black and white Southampton residents. While some white people took comfort in the triumph of the militia, others lived in grief for murdered family members and their shaken grasp on mastery. Black people continued to use the same strategies for everyday resistance and survival that had produced the rebellion. Whites tightened their grip on power and added more patrols. Enslaved and free people of color stole themselves daily and endured.

A century later, when Allen Crawford and other formerly enslaved people remembered the Southampton Rebellion and their enslaved childhoods, they recounted what survivors had passed on to them. In their memory, the rebellion was a warning and a source of pride. They used the phrase "not sharp enough to git by ole Nat" even though they were not old enough to have met Nat Turner.[118] They honored the relatives they were not alive to meet before the rebellion took them away. And they knew what "bugs in the wheat" was code for decades after the slave patrols had ended.[119]

To survive is to both grieve and endure. For African Americans, surviving Southampton did not begin or end with the Southampton Rebellion. The rebellion and the documents that whites produced to make sense of it provide a view of a historical moment when Black people's systems of evasion, resistance, and survival became more visible. These systems were most successful when whites did not detect them or keep records about them. The silences that remain should be trusted and celebrated. An entire community of African Americans, free and enslaved, adults and children, produced the Southampton Rebellion. They daily refashioned sites of labor and oppression into sites of evasion and resistance. Sometimes they endured. Sometimes they met violent ends. But always they mapped new ways to survive.

Conclusion

In July 2015, John Ricks, a retired US marine and Southampton County native, appeared at the county's monthly board of supervisors meeting. Amid public outcry deriding the symbolism of Confederate relics and their complicated place in contemporary public spaces, Ricks came to confront Southampton's violent past. Instead of challenging the place of the county's monument to Confederate Army soldiers and veterans, Ricks had another marker of historical memory and violence in mind. "'I draw my line with the naming of roads," he said. "I don't know who covers the naming of roads, but a month ago I was reading The Washington Post, and it knocked my socks off, gentlemen. I was embarrassed because a paper way out of the state writes an article explaining how Blackhead Signpost Road got its name. I had heard this growing up, but I didn't want to believe it.'"[1]

If you travel to Southampton County today, you will see that its history is written all over its landscape. Its main roads, now paved and marked with state highway labels or green street signs, often follow the routes that they followed in 1831. Many smaller roads in the southern half of the county, the area where most of the rebellion happened, take their names from important sites in the rebellion: Cabin Pond Road, Barrow Road, Porter House Road, and Cross Keys Road are part of the everyday life of the county, imprinted on its Google map, on its street signs, and in the memory of its current residents. Along with these more benign-sounding names was, until recently, a green street sign for Blackhead Signpost Road.

The name Black Head Signpost referred to a significant site of community trauma. Stories vary only slightly about the name's origin. The *Washington Post* article that Ricks referred to in his statement to Southampton's board of supervisors is an op-ed piece written by Alfred L. Brophy titled "Why Northerners Should Support Conferederate [*sic*] Monuments."[2] In the course of his argument that Confederate monuments should remain in public spaces, Brophy explained that Black Head Signpost was named for the severed head of an enslaved Black man that was meant to serve as a warning to other enslaved people with rebellion on their minds. William Sidney Drewry, an early twentieth-century historian of the Southampton Rebellion and a Southampton native, described the origin of the place name thus: "The head of one of the insurgents who had been shot was cut off and stuck on it. It was ever afterwards painted black as a warning against further outrage."[3] Kenneth Greenberg noted in his edited version of *The Confessions of Nat Turner* that "the cavalry company from Murfreesboro decapitated as many as fifteen suspected rebels and placed the heads on poles for display. One head was posted at . . . a crossing which then became known as 'Blackhead Sign Post.'"[4] At least one severed head was on display at the crossroads, and when it decayed the name continued to be used. Ricks said, "I'm asking that Blackhead Signpost Road [be changed.] . . . This is 2015, this is not 1860."[5] In February 2021, in response to a petition, the road's name was changed to Signpost Road. But nearly 184 years after the violent events of August 1831, the county still remains divided about sites of public memory.

But contemporary memory and memorials exist for resistance and survival, not just for pain and violence. Any number of paths and roads on private property connect fields to houses and to county roads. The descendants of Sidney Turner, a farmer and African American resident of the county in the late nineteenth and early twentieth centuries, own one of those paths. The path remains clear mostly due to the efforts of Turner, then his son, and now his grandson. The grandchildren of Sidney and Corrine Turner remember their grandfather walking them down the path past Cabin Pond to a dug-out hole in the ground. There, they were told, is where their ancestor Nat Turner hid out for months after their county's most famous event. There is where he was captured. And there is where Sidney Turner's descendants hoped a proposed Southampton County Historical Society driving tour will make a stop. While plans for a driving tour with physical markers has since been scrapped, an effort to build a digital driving tour led by scholars at Christopher Newport University is going strong, and a downtown walking tour of Courtland, called "Jerusalem in 1831," is a work in progress.

When one of Sidney Turner's granddaughters was asked why the family wanted to make the location a part of a driving tour in 2011, she responded, "We didn't want it to get lost in history. Something really tragic happened here."[6] In the county where America's most famous slave rebellion took place, there are no historical markers to denote where important participants lived and worked, where rebels traveled to visit violence on the white community, or where they were jailed, tried, and hanged. The only marker stands at Cross Keys; it notes that Cross Keys was a crossroads where many whites sought shelter and protection during the rebellion. The historical memory of county residents is vibrant and deeply personal but remains private for many.

It is remarkable that descendants of Nat Turner and Cherry Turner, his wife, own the land on which he was once enslaved, the land where he and his comrades planned out the rebellion, and the land where he hid.[7] It is even more remarkable that Sidney Turner acquired the land in two parcels, one in 1915 and the other in 1939. But the story of the Southampton Rebellion is not just the personal history of one notable enslaved lay preacher. It is also the story of Southampton as a community before, during, and after the intense violence of August 1831. It is, moreover, a contemporary story as well as a historical one. If you visit the county today, its residents refer to the Southampton Rebellion as "the rebellion." The local historical society owns and is restoring Rebecca Vaughn's house, a structure the enslaved rebels visited. The county's website includes a section about the rebellion. But Turner's descendants, who were called upon privately for generations to help curious outsiders locate Nat Turner's cave, did not allow tours led by the local historical society to include their land until 2011. The current owner of the property nearest Cabin Pond has erected his own roadside historical marker to his famous ancestor but does not have one near the family's cave. When the sign was shot through by unidentified vandals, the county replaced it.

Scholars consider the start of the rebellion to be the evening of August 21, 1831, when a group of enslaved men met at Cabin Pond, had a meal, and decided that the next morning they would travel from farm to farm killing every white person they encountered, bolstering their numbers as they went. When the ordeal ended is less concrete in the historiography. For some, the end came sometime in the afternoon of Tuesday, August 23, 1831, when the final skirmish between enslaved rebels and local militia ended. Others claim that it ended about a week later, on Wednesday, August 31, when the first court session convened to pass judgment on the suspected rebels who had managed to survive the violence of the previous week. For many of the county's white residents, the rebellion did not end until a month later, on October 30, when Benjamin Phipps stumbled upon Nat Turner hiding near the farm where he was once enslaved. Regardless of which end date people chose, its moments and dates and places of significance have been determined by the actions and experiences of the rebellion's male participants and the white male survivors who successfully took control of the event's narrative.

For Turner's descendants, who in their 70s decided to share the historical site their family has preserved with their community, the story is not about one of their ancestors; it is about all of them. "This farm is just like our blood," one of them said.[8] For contemporary residents of the county, the story of the rebellion is not the story of the Virginia Debates or the fiery writings of northern abolitionists. It is not the story of one enslaved man's religiosity and journey to leadership. It is the story of their community, their families, and the collective tragedy of the loss of life experienced by all. Now, almost 190 years after the event, some of the descendants of the rebellion's survivors, both white and Black, are making an effort to preserve what was once knowledge in local memory only. The Southampton Rebellion remains a community event that has resonance across racial lines.

In the spring of 2019, as I traveled with a team from Christopher Newport University and Bruce Turner, a descendant of Nat Turner, to map out what might become a digital driving tour, Mr. Turner told stories of his twentieth-century childhood in the county and the lives of his elders and ancestors. We visited the potter's field where most of the remains of those executed in 1831 still lie, a spot from which you can still see the courthouse built on the same spot where the 1831 courthouse stood. We went to the remains of houses and homes that stand in the middle of farmers' fields south of the Nottoway River. We saw the remains of Cypress Bridge, where Turner and his men were first confronted by militia.

When I asked Mr. Turner what his elders had told him about the rebellion, he smiled. "[My grandmother] always told me not to get mixed up in that Turner mess," he replied, chuckling. Much like Allen Crawford, Mr. Turner had been warned. His generous help with the development of the tour, his work to trace his family's history in the archives, and his kinship connections and landownership in the county of course meant that he'd ended up not heeding his grandmother's warning. And his grandmother, who had passed family stories to him, hadn't heeded her own advice and instead had participated in a long tradition of Black women who serve as history keepers and mentors in the arts of survival and resistance. As we packed into our rented SUV to head out of the county, I was awed, as I have been many times over the course of this project, at how alive Black women's strategies of evasion and resistance remain. Mr. Turner's memories brought me closer than the archives could to the voices of Black Southampton women. His grandmother's words served as my final reminder to seek the truth but to trust in silence.

Notes

Author's Note on Language and Sources

1. "Creator, My Heart Speaks," Cheroenhaka (Nottoway) Indian Tribe Official website, https://cheroenhaka-nottoway.org/nottoway-history/heart-speaks.htm.

2. Indian Land is clearly marked on an antebellum map of Virginia that includes Southampton County. It was located just northwest of Jerusalem on the south bank of the Nottoway River. Herman Böÿe, L. V Buchholtz, and Benjamin Tanner, *A Map of the State of Virginia, Constructed in Conformity to Law from the Late Surveys Authorized by the Legislature and Other Original And Authentic Documents* [Virginia: s.n, 1859], https://www.loc.gov/item/99439988/. This plot of land was sometimes called the Circle and Square because of the shape of the reservation. However, the documents I use in this book refer to the reservation as Indian Land. I've used this term so that others can more easily trace my research. See Diane Tennant, "Return of the Natives in Southampton County," Cheroenhaka (Nottoway) Indian Tribe Official website, https://cheroenhaka-nottoway.org/about-nottoway-tribe/return-of-natives-pt-1.htm.

3. P. Gabrielle Forman et al., "Writing about Slavery? Teaching about Slavery? This Might Help," community-sourced document, December 27, 2020, https://docs.google.com/document/d/1A4TEdDgYslX-hlKezLodMIM71My3KTNozxRvoIQTOQs/mobilebasic.

Prologue

1. Charles L. Perdue Jr., Thomas E. Barden, and Robert K. Phillips, eds., *Weevils in the Wheat: Interviews with Virginia Ex-Slaves* (Charlottesville: University of Virginia Press, 1991), 75.

2. Perdue, Barden, and Phillips, *Weevils in the Wheat*, 167.

3. Perdue, Barden, and Phillips, *Weevils in the Wheat*, 75.

Introduction

1. Nat Turner, *The Confessions of Nat Turner and Related Documents*, edited and with an introduction by Kenneth S. Greenberg (Boston: Bedford Books of St. Martin's Press, 1996), 48–49.

2. Turner, *The Confessions of Nat Turner*, 48–49.

3. Turner, *The Confessions of Nat Turner*, 57.

4. Turner, *The Confessions of Nat Turner*, 7.

5. See Herbert Aptheker, *American Negro Slave Revolts*, 5th ed. (New York: International Publishers, 1983); Stephanie M. H. Camp, *Closer to Freedom: Enslaved Women and Everyday Resistance in the Plantation South* (Chapel Hill: University of North Carolina Press, 2004); Sylviane A. Diouf, *Slavery's Exiles: The Story of the American Maroons* (2014; repr., New York: New York University Press, 2016); Douglas R. Egerton, *Gabriel's Rebellion: The Virginia Slave Conspiracies of 1800 and 1802* (Chapel Hill: University of North Carolina Press, 1993); Douglas R. Egerton, *He Shall Go Out Free: The Lives of Denmark Vesey*, rev. ed. (Lanham, MD: Rowman & Littlefield, 2004); and James Sidbury, *Ploughshares into Swords: Race, Rebellion, and Identity in Gabriel's Virginia, 1730–1810* (New York: Cambridge University Press, 1997). See also Junius P. Rodriguez, *Encyclopedia of Slave Resistance and Rebellion*, 2 vols., Greenwood Milestones in African American History (Westport, CT: Greenwood, 2006).

6. French's work on Nat Turner as both a historical figure and a racial archetype demonstrates the cultural significance of the Southampton Rebellion and Nat Turner during the nineteenth century and beyond. Scot French, *The Rebellious Slave: Nat Turner in American Memory* (Boston: Houghton Mifflin Harcourt, 2004).

7. Anthony E. Kaye, *Joining Places: Slave Neighborhoods in the Old South* (Chapel Hill: University of North Carolina Press, 2009).

8. Camp, *Closer to Freedom*. Camp's work is in direct conversation with both the foundational works and more contemporaneous works on American slave rebellion such as Egerton, *Gabriel's Rebellion*; Sidbury, *Ploughshares into Swords*; and Kenneth Greenberg, ed., *Nat Turner: A Slave Rebellion in History and Memory* (New York: Oxford University Press, 2004).

9. Turner, *The Confessions of Nat Turner*, 11–14.

10. For examples of women's roles as laborers, mothers, and community members, see Deborah Gray White, *Ar'n't I a Woman? Female Slaves in the Plantation South* (New York: W. W. Norton, 1985); Jacqueline Jones, *Labor of Love, Labor of Sorrow: Black Women, Work, and the Family, from Slavery to the Present* (New York: Basic Books, 1985); Leslie A. Schwalm, *A Hard Fight for We: Women's Transition from Slavery to Freedom in South Carolina* (Urbana: University of Illinois Press, 1997); Tera W. Hunter, *To 'Joy My Freedom: Southern Black Women's Lives and Labors After the Civil War* (Cambridge, MA: Harvard University Press, 1998); and Judith A. Carney, *Black Rice: The African Origins of Rice Cultivation in the Americas* (Cambridge, MA: Harvard University Press, 2002).

11. David F. Allmendinger Jr., *Nat Turner and the Rising in Southampton County* (2014; repr., Baltimore: Johns Hopkins University Press, 2017); Patrick H. Breen, *The Land Shall Be Deluged in Blood: A New History of the Nat Turner Revolt* (New York: Oxford University Press, 2016). Recently, Patrick Breen has used trial records to explicate the motivations and trace the actions of white Southampton residents during the trials, which lasted from late August through November of 1831. Similarly, Allmendinger has used trial records to illuminate the many connections between whites in the community. Both assert that whites used the trials to project and practice mastery, to reassert their power over enslaved people, and to record their efforts to define civility and their proper place at the top of their slave society's hierarchy. Neither argued that the trials were about justice or the truth of the rebellion's events. I agree with these interpretations.

Chapter 1. Geographies of Surveillance and Control

1. Camp, *Closer to Freedom*, 16.

2. The contemporary Cheroenhaka regard the name Nottoway to be a derogatory anglicization of an Algonquin name for their people. They refer to themselves as Cheroenhaka (Nottoway) in their writings about themselves. See Red Hawk "Teerheer," "Creator, My Heart Speaks," https://cheroenhaka-nottoway.org/nottoway-history/heart-speaks.htm.

3. Thomas C. Parramore, *Southampton County, Virginia* (Charlottesville: Published for the Southampton County Historical Society by the University Press of Virginia, 1978), 1–19. See also Arica L. Coleman, *That the Blood Stay Pure: African Americans, Native Americans, and the Predicament of Race and Identity in Virginia* (Bloomington: Indiana University Press, 2013), 219–224. See also Herman Böÿe, L. V. Buchholtz, and Benjamin Tanner, *A Map of the State of Virginia, Constructed in Conformity to Law from the Late Surveys Authorized by the Legislature and Other Original and Authentic Documents* [Virginia: s.n, 1859], https://www.loc.gov/item/99439988/, which shows Indian Land just northwest of Jerusalem on the southern bank of the Nottoway River.

4. Parramore, *Southampton County, Virginia*, 28–29.

5. Rupert B. Vance, *Human Factors in Cotton Culture: A Study in the Social Geography of the American South* (Chapel Hill: University of North Carolina Press, 1929), 14.

6. Turner, *The Confessions of Nat Turner*, 6–7.

7. The accepted metric is usually that farms with twenty enslaved laborers constituted a plantation. Census records for the Cross Keys neighborhood indicate that most farmers enslaved between ten and fifteen people.

8. University of Virginia, Historical Census Browser, 1790 and 1800, https://mapserver.lib.virginia.edu/. This now-defunct database enabled users to compare the total population of various groups over time at county and state levels. The librarians at the University of Virginia recommend another site, https://www.socialexplorer.com/, which performs those functions and more. However, Social Explorer is behind a paywall.

9. Aptheker, *American Negro Slave Revolts*, 13.

10. Camp, *Closer to Freedom*, 16.

11. Camp, *Closer to Freedom*, 12.

12. For studies of the development of slave societies in the Chesapeake and Virginia, see Ira Berlin, *Many Thousands Gone: The First Two Centuries of Slavery in North America* (Cambridge, Mass.: Belknap Press, 2000); and Edmund S. Morgan, *American Slavery, American Freedom: The Ordeal of Colonial Virginia* (1975; repr., New York: W. W. Norton & Company, 2003).

13. Sally E. Hadden, *Slave Patrols: Law and Violence in Virginia and the Carolinas* (Cambridge, MA: Harvard University Press, 2003), 6–41.

14. William Waller Hening, *The New Virginia Justice: Comprising the Office and Authority of a Justice of the Peace, in the Commonwealth of Virginia. Together with a Variety of Useful Precedents, Adapted to the Laws Now in Force. To Which Is Added, an Appendix, Containing All the Most Approved Forms in Conveyancing: Such as Deeds of Bargain and Sale, of Lease and Release; of Trust, Mortgages, Bills of Sale, &c. Also, the Duties of a Justice of the Peace, Arising Under the Laws of the United States* (Johnson & Warner, 1810), 543. Virginia legislators did not enact laws regulating the trials of enslaved people until the 1690s, many years after enslaved people were introduced into the colony. Such trials were handled in courts of oyer and terminer by a panel of justices, not a jury.

15. For a careful study of the development of slave law and definitions of slave crime in Virginia, see Philip J. Schwarz, *Twice Condemned: Slaves and the Criminal Laws of Virginia* (Baton Rouge: Louisiana State University Press, 1988). For early national and antebellum legal cultural history and the importance of custom and hierarchy over concepts of rights, see Laura F. Edwards, *The People and Their Peace: Legal Culture and the Transformation of Inequality in the Post-Revolutionary South* (Chapel Hill: University of North Carolina Press, 2009).

16. Hadden, *Slave Patrols*, 24–32.

17. Berlin, *Many Thousands Gone*; Kathleen M. Brown, *Good Wives, Nasty Wenches, and Anxious Patriarchs: Gender, Race, and Power in Colonial Virginia* (Chapel Hill: University of North Carolina Press, 1996); Edmund S. Morgan, *American Slavery, American Freedom*; Philip D. Morgan, *Slave Counterpoint: Black Culture in the Eighteenth-Century Chesapeake and Lowcountry* (Chapel Hill: Omohundro Institute and University of North Carolina Press, 1998).

18. Hadden, *Slave Patrols*, 24–32.

19. Berlin, *Many Thousands Gone*, 109–141. Berlin's fifth chapter provides an excellent overview of Virginia's development as a tobacco colony and a slave society.

20. Berlin, *Many Thousands Gone*, 29. While Virginians experimented with many laws in an effort to discourage rebellion beginning in the seventeenth century, patrols grew out of an expansion of the militia's duties in the early eighteenth century. Militias and the patrols culled from them were meant to discourage enslaved people's meetings, not to prohibit slaves from being mobile. Passes were meant to allow for enslaved people's mobility in service to the needs of their enslavers.

21. Hadden, *Slave Patrols*, 28–32.

22. Henry Irving Tragle, *The Southampton Slave Revolt of 1831: A Compilation of Source Material, Including the Full Text of the Confessions of Nat Turner* (New York: Vintage Books, 1973), 17.

23. Tragle, *The Southampton Slave Revolt of 1831*, 17.

24. Bertram Wyatt-Brown, *Honor and Violence in the Old South* (New York: Oxford, 1986), 146–147. Wyatt-Brown's work illustrates the importance of militia activity and rank to the social status of white males. He also demonstrates the importance of violence against other white men and enslaved people as a means of establishing and maintaining white norms of masculinity.

25. Hadden, *Slave Patrols*, 41–47.

26. Hadden, *Slave Patrols*, 73. Hadden asserts that slave patrols consisted of men of all classes who were eligible for militia service, demonstrating the fallacy of the common myth that only poor whites served as patrollers. This allowed for cross-class racial and gendered bonding and preserved social hierarchies. The wealthy often served as officers over men who were less well off.

27. Slave Patrol Records, 1754–1859, Box 2, Folder 2, Southampton County (Va.) Free Negro and Slave Records, 1754–1860, Library of Virginia, Richmond (hereafter Slave Patrol Records).

Extant documents relating to the presence of militias and patrols in antebellum Southampton County for the period 1795 to 1860 provide a clearer picture of what those who chose to rebel in 1831 may have perceived as a possible threat to success. However, while the 1810s and 1820 are well represented, no documents are available for the period 1821 to 1860. Also, the content of the documents varies widely. Some patrol leaders handed the court clerk well-organized, clearly written charts that include dates, names, and the hours a unit spent patrolling. Others simply turned in small scraps of paper for individual patrol members that contain no record of where or when they patrolled. It is possible to piece together who participated in individual patrol groups, but the boundaries of each group's militia remain obscure. With further study, patrol areas may become clearer. What the documents do reveal are some of the patterns of patrolling present in the county during the period that rebellion participants were children and young adults. They indicate local responses to threats of violence that participants in the rebellion may have remembered from their adolescence and young adulthood. Though imperfect, these sources give significant insight into an important system of surveillance in antebellum Southampton County.

28. "An Act for Regulating and Disciplining the Militia," May 1777, in *The Statutes at Large, Being a Collection of All the Laws of Virginia, from the First Session of the Legislature in the Year 1619*, vol. 9 (Richmond: J. and G. Cochran, 1821), 278.

29. Slave Patrol Records. Patrols were instructed to deliver truants to a justice of the peace.

30. Tragle, *The Southampton Slave Revolt*, 15.

31. Slave Patrol Records.

32. Slave Patrol Records.

33. Patrol Orders, June 7 and 9, 1810, Slave Patrol Records.

34. Thomas Hanley, patrol reports, June 9 and June 16, 1810, Slave Patrol Records.

35. Richard Marby, patrol reports, June 10, 12, and 16, 1810, and October 1810, Slave Patrol Records.

36. Richard Marby, patrol reports, January and February 1811, Slave Patrol Records.

37. Perdue, Barden, and Phillips, *Weevils in the Wheat*, 190. The heavy presence of slave patrols in the narratives of the formerly enslaved persons the Works Progress Administration interviewed in the mid-twentieth century may be the result of the age of most interviewees. Many, if not all, were children at the time of their enslavement. Their fear of slave patrols may have derived from the stories adults told them about the brutality of the patrollers.

38. Perdue, Barden, and Phillips, *Weevils in the Wheat*, 155.

39. Perdue, Barden, and Phillips, *Weevils in the Wheat*, 75.

40. Perdue, Barden, and Phillips, *Weevils in the Wheat*, 34.

41. Perdue, Barden, and Phillips, *Weevils in the Wheat*, 299.

42. Perdue, Barden, and Phillips, *Weevils in the Wheat*, 93, 141.

43. Perdue, Barden, and Phillips, *Weevils in the Wheat*, 93, 157, 214–215.

44. Perdue, Barden, and Phillips, *Weevils in the Wheat*, 75.

45. Perdue, Barden, and Phillips, *Weevils in the Wheat*, 220.

46. Perdue, Barden, and Phillips, *Weevils in the Wheat*, 220.

47. Perdue, Barden, and Phillips, *Weevils in the Wheat*, 180.

Chapter 2. Enslaved Women and Strategies of Evasion and Resistance

1. Moting is the process of hand cleaning cotton by picking out small pieces of cotton seed left behind in cotton fiber after it has been ginned.

2. Allmendinger, *Nat Turner and the Rising in Southampton County*, 77.

3. I first learned of Charlotte and Ester in William Sidney Drewry, *The Southampton Insurrection* (Washington, DC: Neale Company, 1900), 47–48. For more contemporary retellings, see also Allmendinger, *Nat Turner and the Rising in Southampton County*, 281–282; and Breen, *The Land Shall Be Deluged in Blood*, 52–53.

4. Drewry, *The Southampton Insurrection*, 47–48.

5. In 1830, Thomas Ridley, a prominent resident of the county, enslaved 145 people. Image of 1830 federal manuscript census record for Thomas Ridley, NARA Record Group 29, microfilm publication M19, reel 196, page 243, accessed on Ancestry.com.

6. Southampton County (Va.) Free Negro and Slave Records, 1754–1860, Library of Virginia, Richmond (hereafter Free Negro and Slave Records). My characterization of the two parishes draws upon my analysis of the 1830 federal manuscript census and on the analysis of that census in Turner, *The Confessions of Nat Turner*, 6–7; and Tragle, *The Southampton Slave Revolt of 1831*, 13–16.

7. Francis Family Bible Record, 1805–1929, Library of Virginia, image at http://image.lva.virginia.gov/BibleII/35575.pdf.

8. According to photographic evidence and the 1830 federal census, Salathiel lived in a small hut with seven enslaved people. "Home of Salathiel Francis," Speech and Photographs Relating to Nat Turner's Insurrection, University of Virginia Library, Charlottesville, https://ead.lib.virginia.edu/vivaxtf/view?docId=uva-sc/viu01760.xml; and image of 1830 federal manuscript census record for Selathan [Salathiel] Francis, NARA Record Group 29, microfilm publication M19, reel 196, page 260, accessed on Ancestry.com.

9. Image of 1830 federal manuscript census record for Nathaniel Francis, NARA Record Group 29, microfilm publication M19, reel 196, page 259.

10. I consider working age to be the second available age category for enslaved people (10 to 24 and older), although children much younger than 10 were used for agricultural tasks.

11. "Free Negro Lists, Determined Insolvent, Delinquent, or Non-Inhabitants, 1791–1860," Lists of Free Negroes, Nottoway Parish, 1817, 1821, 1822, 1826, box 2, folder 2, Free Negro and Slave Records; "Apprentice and Indenture of Colored Children, 1820–1859", box 2, folder 2, Free Negro and Slave Records. The Free Negro and Slave Records collection includes records for free people of color in St. Luke's Parish in the 1820s. Each document lists the name, place of residence, and occupation of each person of working age. Free women are almost universally listed as spinsters. Indentures for free girls of color indicate that they were trained to perform domestic/housekeeping labor, not field work.

12. Daina Ramey Berry, *"Swing the Sickle for the Harvest Is Ripe": Gender and Slavery in Antebellum Georgia* (Urbana: University of Illinois Press, 2007), 24–28. Berry discusses the perception that enslaved laborers, especially women, were skilled at harvesting cotton. She demonstrates throughout her book that skill, rather than gender, is what made a person a full hand.

13. Perdue, Barden, and Phillips, *Weevils in the Wheat*, 199.

14. Perdue, Barden, and Phillips, *Weevils in the Wheat*, 199.

15. Perdue, Barden, and Phillips, *Weevils in the Wheat*, 199.

16. Perdue, Barden, and Phillips, *Weevils in the Wheat*, 199.

17. Perdue, Barden, and Phillips, *Weevils in the Wheat*, 148.

18. Carney, *Black Rice*; Berry, *"Swing the Sickle for the Harvest Is Ripe,"* 24–28.

19. Barbara Bush, *Slave Women in Caribbean Society, 1650–1838* (Bloomington: Indiana University Press, 1990).

20. Free Negro Register, Nottoway Parish, 1821–23, Nottoway Parish 1826, and Free Negro Registry, St. Luke's Parish, 1822, Free Negro and Slave Records.

21. Victor S. Clark, *History of Manufactures in the United States, 1607–1860* (Washington, DC: Carnegie Institution of Washington, 1916), 319.

22. Clark, *History of Manufactures in the United States*, 439–440.

23. Tragle, *The Southampton Slave Revolt of 1831*, 208.

24. Tragle, *The Southampton Slave Revolt of 1831*, 194–195.

25. Trial of Jack and Andrew, September 1, 1831, Southampton County Court Minute Book, 1830–1835, pages 74–76, Southampton County (Va.) County Records Collection, Court Records, reel 34, Library of Virginia, Richmond. See also Tragle, *The Southampton Slave Revolt of 1831*, 179–182.

26. Drewry, *The Southampton Insurrection*, 60. Drewry notes that dinner was "then preparing" in the kitchen Cynthia was in when rebels arrived at the farm where she was enslaved.

27. Drewry, *The Southampton Insurrection*, 85.

Chapter 3. Free Issues

1. Tragle, *The Southampton Slave Revolt of 1831*, 202, 235.

2. Tragle, *The Southampton Slave Revolt of 1831*, 203.

3. Luther Porter Jackson, *Free Negro Labor and Property Holding in Virginia, 1830–1860* (New York: Appleton, 1942); Melvin Patrick Ely, *Israel on the Appomattox: A Southern Experiment in Black Freedom from the 1790s through the Civil War* (New York: Knopf, 2004); and Ira Berlin, *Slaves without Masters: The Free Negro in the Antebellum South* (1974; repr., New York: New Press, 2007).

4. Suzanne Lebsock, *The Free Women of Petersburg: Status and Culture in a Southern Town, 1784–1860* (New York: Norton, 1985), 90–92. Lebsock's chapter on free women of color outlines the shifting legal status of free people of color in Virginia before the Southampton Rebellion.

5. In a chapter titled "Fear of Insurrection," Harriet Jacobs notes how poorly free people of color were treated in the wake of the rebellion. Harriet A. Jacobs, *Incidents in the Life of a Slave Girl: Written by Herself* (Chapel Hill: University of North Carolina at Chapel Hill, 1860).

6. For a full history of the Virginia debates, see Erik S. Root, *Sons of the Fathers: The Virginia Slavery Debates of 1831–2* (Lanham, MD: Lexington Books, 2010). See also Ely, *Israel on the Appomattox*, 5–15, 175–224; and Charles F. Irons, *The Origins of Proslavery Christianity: White and Black Evangelicals in Colonial and Antebellum Virginia* (Chapel Hill: University of North Carolina Press, 2008), 133–168.

7. Virginia General Assembly, House of Delegates, "Bill No. 13," in *Journal of the House of Delegates of the Commonwealth of Virginia, Begun and Held at the Capitol, in the City of Richmond, on Monday, the Fifth Day of December, One Thousand Eight Hundred and Thirty-One* (Richmond: Thomas Ritchie, 1831), 1–8. This draft bill presented to the House of Delegates in 1831 included rules to restrict the movement of free Black people and named removal from Virginia as punishment for Black people who did not comply with the law. After a lengthy debate, Virginia's legislators voted against a bill to gradually manumit enslaved people in the commonwealth and a bill to remove free people. In that session, the legislature passed a law that prohibited free people who did not plan to emigrate to Libera from practicing trades and one that barred free Black people from preaching. See also Root, *Sons of the Fathers*.

8. Perdue, Barden, and Phillips, *Weevils in the Wheat*, 53.

9. William W. Hening, *The New Virginia Justice* (Richmond, [VA]: August Davis, 1794), 540, 549–550; "An Act to Amend the Act, Intituled [*sic*] An Act, to Reduce into One the Several Acts, Concerning Slaves, Free Negroes and Mulattoes," in Samuel Shepherd, ed., *The Statutes at Large of Virginia, from October Session 1792, to December Session 1806, Inclusive, in Three Volumes, (New Series), Being a Continuation of Hening* (Richmond: Samuel Shepherd, 1835), 1:363–365. The act, which passed on December 25, 1795, explicitly stated that free and enslaved people could be witnesses only in commonwealth cases that involved only other free Blacks or enslaved people.

10. Berlin, *Slaves without Masters*.

11. Berlin, *Slaves without Masters*, 187.

12. Perdue, Barden, and Phillips, *Weevils in the Wheat*, 137.

13. Ely, *Israel on the Appomattox*, 5–15, 175–224.

14. A 1793 law mandated this practice: "All free negroes and mulattoes, residing in towns, to be registered and numbered, in a book to be kept by the clerk; with register shall specify the age, name, colour and stature, by some and in what court emancipated, or whether born free. A copy of the register, signed by the clerk and attested by one alderman, to be annually delivered to the negro or mulatto, by the clerk, at a fee of twenty-five cents." Amendments to the act in the early nineteenth century required new forms of proof of freedom from previous residences, but the fees and practices remained the same. See Hening, *The New Virginia Justice* (1794), 546, 551.

15. According to the 1793 law, free people of color were not permitted to be at large in communities unless they were registered at the county courthouse. A revision to this code in 1805 expanded this stipulation to allow whites to apprehend any free person of color who was found in a county where he or she was not registered and could not produce proof of employment on demand. Hening, *The New Virginia Justice* (1794), 546–547, 555.

16. Registry for St. Luke's Parish, 1822, and registries for Nottoway Parish, 1821 and 1826, Free Negro and Slave Records. The registries available for the 1820s reveal a variety of living arrangements. Notably, St. Luke's Parish included the site of the county's Indian reservation, often called simply Indian Land.

17. Registry for St. Luke's Parish, 1822, and registries for Nottoway Parish, 1821 and 1826, Free Negro and Slave Records.

18. Registry for St. Luke's Parish, 1822, and registries for Nottoway Parish, 1821 and 1826. The registers did not make any distinction between the two groups.

19. Jackson, *Free Negro Labor and Property Holding in Virginia*, 34. Jackson provides a detailed description of Virginia's position in the political and economic life of the United States in the early nineteenth century. He notes how soil exhaustion, white outmigration, and the expense of enslaved laborers left a labor niche for free people of color first in rural and later in urban contexts in Virginia.

20. Jackson, *Free Negro Labor and Property Holding in Virginia*, 72.

21. Registry for St. Luke's Parish, 1822.

22. Registry for St. Luke's Parish, 1822.

23. Free people of color appear throughout the 1830 federal manuscript census for the neighborhood that was most affected by the rebellion.

24. Tragle, *The Southampton Slave Revolt of 1831*, xvi.

25. Image of 1830 federal manuscript census record for Jacob Williams, NARA Record Group 29, microfilm publication M19, reel 196, page 259, accessed on Ancestry.com.

26. Image of 1830 federal manuscript census record for Jacob Williams.

27. Image of 1830 federal manuscript census record for Edwin Barns, NARA Record Group 29, microfilm publication M19, reel 196, page 260, accessed on Ancestry.com.

28. Image of 1830 federal manuscript census record for Richard Porter, NARA Record Group 29, microfilm publication M19, reel 196, page 256, accessed on Ancestry.com.

29. Ester, one of the enslaved women used for domestic labor, did not join the household until late in 1830. She may have made the free woman redundant, or she may have been at the exclusive beck and call of Lavinia Francis, who brought her into the household when she married.

30. Historical Census Browser, University of Virginia, Geospatial and Statistical Data Center, http://mapserver.lib.virginia.edu/.

31. "A List of Free Negroes and Mulattoes in the County of Southampton and Parish of St. Luke's, May 1807, page 3, folder "1803 St. Lukes," Southampton County, Free Negro Lists, 1801–1831, Free Negro and Slave Records.

32. Cosby's household is listed in the Free Negro Registry for St. Luke's Parish in 1822 and he is listed as a head of household in the 1820 census; image of 1820 federal manuscript census record for Jonas Cosby, NARA Record Group 29, microfilm publication M33, reel 142, page 114, accessed on Ancestry.com.

33. Coleman, *That the Blood Stay Pure*, 81.

34. Coleman, *That the Blood Stay Pure*, 222.

35. Coleman, *That the Blood Stay Pure*, 221.

36. These groups include heterosexual couples and their biological children. This registry does not provide information about informal kinship relationships or extended biological family and does not indicate how household residences were organized. Box 2, folder "List of Free Negroes within the District of A. Middleton, Commissioner for St. Luke's Parish, 1822," Free Negro and Slave Records.

37. Married women are listed only as Mrs. followed by their husband's surname. This does not mean that the women listed as single were not married. They may have been married to enslaved men who could not legally marry.

38. Perdue, Barden, and Phillips, *Weevils in the Wheat*, 90.

39. "List of Free Negroes within the District of A. Middleton Commissioner for St. Luke's Parish," 1822, box 2, folder 2, Free Negro and Slave Records.

40. It is possible that this Stephen is the same man officials listed as Stephen Barham, a shoemaker, in the Free Negro and Slave Records. "List of Free Negroes

and Mulattoes in Nottoway Parish in the County of Southampton for 1826 by Benj. Griffin C. Revenue," 1826, box 2, folder 2, Free Negro and Slave Records.

41. In 1822, 88 percent of free men of color in St. Luke's Parish were listed as farmers. Only three men of the remaining 12 percent listed a skilled trade as their occupation: two were shoemakers and one was a tailor. "List of Free Negroes within the District of A. Middleton, Commissioner for St. Luke's Parish," 1822, box 2, folder 2, Free Negro and Slave Records.

42. "List of Free Negroes within the District of A. Middleton, Commissioner for St. Luke's Parish," 1822, box 2, folder 2, Free Negro and Slave Records. The record for Patty Jordan is smeared, but it appears that she lived with a free Black man and another couple, all with the same last name. She was either married to George Jordan or related to him.

43. I use the term "master" here in reference to the adult in charge of bound children. This was the term used in cases of apprenticeship and indenture.

44. "List of Free Negroes within the District of A. Middleton, Commissioner for St. Luke's Parish," 1822, box 2, folder 2, Free Negro and Slave Records.

45. "List of Free Negroes within the District of A. Middleton, Commissioner for St. Luke's Parish," 1822, box 2, folder 2, Free Negro and Slave Records.

46. The Oxford English Dictionary traces the history of the word *spinster* and its various meanings in the English language. OED online, accessed February 1, 2019.

47. Mrs. Georgina Gibbs remembered that enslaved women worked in a special loom house to produce cloth for enslaved people's clothing. Perdue, Barden, and Phillips, *Weevils in the Wheat*, 104.

48. Allmendinger, *Nat Turner and the Rising in Southampton County*, 289–299.

49. Nat Turner, *The Confessions of Nat Turner*, 19. See also Stephen B. Oates, *The Fires of Jubilee: Nat Turner's Fierce Rebellion* (1975; repr., New York: Harper-Collins, 2016), 99–100. Oates describes how two columns of cavalry in this unit murdered more than forty African Americans while patrolling the county after the rebellion. Using local tax records, David Allmendinger Jr. disputes claims of high levels of violence after the rebellion; see Allmendinger, *Nat Turner and the Rising in Southampton County*, 289–299.

50. Tragle, *The Southampton Slave Revolt of 1831*, 203. See also trial of Hardy, September 7, 1831, Southampton County Court Minute Book, 1830–1835, Southampton County (Va.) County Records Collection, Court Records, reel 34, pages 96–99, Library of Virginia, Richmond.

51. Tragle, *The Southampton Slave Revolt*, 234–243. Newsom was a free Black apprentice of Peter Edwards; see Drewry, *The Southampton Insurrection*, 158; and Allmendinger, *Nat Turner and the Rising in Southampton County*, 202. For information on the apprentice system, see Hening, *The New Virginia Justice* (1794), 63–68.

52. Turner, *The Confessions of Nat Turner*, 18–19.

53. Tragle, *The Southampton Slave Revolt*, 190–191.

54. Alejandro de la Fuente and Ariela J. Gross, *Becoming Free, Becoming Black: Race, Freedom, and Law in Cuba, Virginia, and Louisiana* (Cambridge: Cambridge University Press, 2020), 132–177.

55. De la Fuente and Gross, *Becoming Free, Becoming Black*, 132–177. See also Ely, *Israel on the Appomattox*, 175–224.

56. Jacobs, *Incidents in the Life of a Slave Girl*, 97.

57. Parramore, *Southampton County, Virginia*, 115–116.

58. Image of 1840 federal manuscript census record for Nathaniel Francis, NARA Record Group 29, microfilm publication M704, reel 575, page 94, accessed on Ancestry.com.

Chapter 4. Generation, Resistance, and Survival

1. For example, Salathiel Francis, a nearby neighbor, housed himself and seven slaves in a small cabin. Thomas Ridley, who lived a few miles to the northwest of the Travis farm, had a slave quarter that would later serve as a hideout for Nat Turner and his army. Image of 1830 federal manuscript census record for Salathiel Francis; image of 1830 federal manuscript census record for Thomas Ridley, NARA Record Group 29, microfilm publication M19, reel 196, pages 243 and 259, respectively, accessed on Ancestry.com. See also Allmendinger, *Nat Turner and the Rising in Southampton County*, 92, 105.

2. For more on plantation and farm yards and the importance of the kitchen as a site of labor and social activity, see John Michael Vlach, *Back of the Big House: The Architecture of Plantation Slavery* (Chapel Hill: University of North Carolina Press, 1993), 43–62.

3. Breen, *The Land Shall Be Deluged in Blood*, 28.

4. For an account of the Travis murders, see Turner, *The Confessions of Nat Turner*.

5. Tragle, *The Southampton Slave Revolt of 1831*, 96.

6. In his confessions, Nat Turner traced his spiritual journey toward leading the Southampton Rebellion to his early childhood. While he notes years of personal preparation, he marks the solar eclipse of February 12, 1831, as the time that he decided to begin planning with Henry, Hark, Nelson, and Sam. These men and Will and Jack attended the Cabin Pond meeting late on August 21, 1831, where they decided that it was time to launch the rebellion they had plotted since the previous winter. July 4, 1831, was the original date the group set, but bad weather forced them to postpone. Turner, *The Confessions of Nat Turner*, 44–48, 134.

7. Tragle, *The Southampton Slave Revolt of 1831*, 220–221.

8. Nat Turner remained missing from August 23 to October 30, 1831; Oates, *The Fires of Jubilee*. See also Turner, *The Confessions of Nat Turner*, 54–55; and Allmendinger, *Nat Turner and the Rising in Southampton County*, 240–241.

9. The narrative most historians tell of the Southampton Rebellion centers enslaved men. Because enslavers produced a male-centered narrative to downplay the impact and reach of the rebellion, enslaved women, enslaved children, and free people of color rarely appear. Patrick Breen's recent work addresses this issue; see *The Land Shall Be Deluged in Blood*. See also Turner, *The Confessions of Nat Turner*, 37–58. For narratives of the Southampton Rebellion, see Allmendinger, *Nat Turner and the Rising in Southampton County*; Aptheker, *American Negro Slave*

Revolts; Drewry, *The Southampton Insurrection*; Oates, *The Fires of Jubilee*; Parramore, *Southampton County, Virginia*; Tragle, *The Southampton Slave Revolt of 1831*; Egerton, *Gabriel's Rebellion*; Egerton, *He Shall Go Out Free*; Daniel Rasmussen, *American Uprising: The Untold Story of America's Largest Slave Revolt* (New York: Harper Perennial, 2012); David Robertson, *Denmark Vesey: The Buried Story of America's Largest Slave Rebellion and the Man Who Led It* (New York: Vintage, 2000); Sidbury, *Ploughshares into Swords*; and Camp, *Closer to Freedom*. Additionally, in "'What Happened in This Place'? In Search of the Female Slave in the Nat Turner Slave Insurrection," Mary Kemp Davis investigates the participation of women in the Southampton Rebellion. In Greenberg, *Nat Turner*, 162–176.

10. I use the term *children* to denote persons age of 13 and under. I use the term *infant* for children under the age of one year. I use the term *youths* to denote individuals in their teens. White adults referred to the young people I refer to in this chapter as boys, not as teens or youths. White adults involved in the court proceedings noted their ages as outside the category of adult. This categorization was in service to the court's valuation of enslaved defendants, but it may have figured into the court's judgments in each case. Determining the ages of enslaved people and the cultural meaning of their ages can be difficult, especially at the intersection of paternalist racism and various kinds of abuse. For more on enslaved peoples' ages and their changing monetary value, see Daina Ramey Berry, *The Price for Their Pound of Flesh: The Value of the Enslaved, from Womb to Grave, in the Building of a Nation* (New York: Beacon Press, 2017).

11. Aptheker, *American Negro Slave Revolts*; Vincent Harding, *There Is a River: The Black Struggle for Freedom in America* (New York: Mariner Books, 1993).

12. John W. Blassingame, *The Slave Community: Plantation Life in the Antebellum South*, rev. and enlarged ed. (New York: Oxford University Press, 1979); Eugene D. Genovese, *Roll, Jordan, Roll: The World the Slaves Made* (New York: Vintage, 1976); Herbert G. Gutman, *The Black Family in Slavery and Freedom, 1750–1925* (New York: Vintage, 1977).

13. Tragle, *The Southampton Slave Revolt of 1831*. The original Southampton County Court Minute Books for the period 1830–1835 are in the Southampton County (Va.) County Records Collection at the Library of Virginia, Richmond. PDF files of the court minute books can be accessed at The Brantley Association of America's online archive produced in cooperation with the Southampton County clerk at http://www.brantleyassociation.com/southampton_project/southampton _project_list.htm. I have used Tragle's transcription of court records in *The Southampton Slave Revolt of 1831*.

14. Tragle, *The Southampton Slave Revolt of 1831*, 199–201, 211, 220–221.

15. For the compensation of enslavers when those they enslaved were sentenced to death or to sale out of state, see Hening, *The New Virginia Justice* (1810 edition), 543, 549.

16. Image of 1830 federal manuscript census for Southampton Parish, Virginia, NARA Record Group 29, microfilm publication M19, reel 196, accessed on Ancestry.com.

17. Image of 1830 federal manuscript census record for Joseph Travis, NARA Record Group 29, microfilm publication M19, reel 196, pages 259–260, accessed on Ancestry.com. "Joseph Travis," October 5, 1892, Virginia, U.S., Select Marriages, 1785–1940, Ancestry.com, [database online], Provo, UT, USA, Ancestry.com Operations, Inc., 2014.

18. For extensive discussion of the kinship network between the Francis and Travis families, see Allmendinger, *Nat Turner and the Rising in Southampton County*, 44–86.

19. Image of 1830 manuscript census record for Catharine Whitehead, NARA Record Group 29, microfilm publication M19, reel 196, page 260.

20. Wilma King, *Stolen Childhood: Slave Youth in Nineteenth-Century America*, 2nd ed. (Bloomington: Indiana University Press, 2011). King's landmark study augments earlier community studies by demonstrating the value of children to parents, kin, and adults. See also Marie Jenkins Schwartz, *Born in Bondage: Growing Up Enslaved in the Antebellum South* (Cambridge, MA: Harvard University Press, 2001). Instead of seeing children as symbols of a future of slavery or freedom for adults or within adult constructions of community, both scholars read the history of slavery as including children as actors. Looking at the intersection of adult perceptions, ideas, and dreams for their progeny with the actions and experiences of enslaved children is an important method for recovering the lives of enslaved children and their free counterparts.

21. King, *Stolen Childhood*, 71. King's chapter "'Us ain't never idle': The Work of Enslaved Children and Youth" details the many ways enslavers and those in charge of bound children used them to accomplish a range of tasks, including those usually performed by adults.

22. Berlin, *Many Thousands Gone*. Berlin provides extensive information on the development of the gang system of labor over generations in British North America, with the exception of the Carolina Low Country, where the task system was favored. See also Brenda E. Stevenson, *Life in Black and White: Family and Community in the Slave South* (New York: Oxford University Press, 1996), 190–193. Stevenson covers the use of the gang system in the tobacco fields of antebellum Virginia.

23. King, *Stolen Childhood*.

24. Apprentice Indentures for Free Negroes (1820–1860), box 2, folder 2, Free Negro and Slave Records, 1754–1860, Southampton County Court Records, Library of Virginia, Richmond (hereafter Library of Virginia).

25. Hening, *The New Virginia Justice* (1794), 66–68; For example, justices of the peace ordered overseers of the poor to bind out free children of color. See "Apprenticeship Order for Adolphus Whitehead, October 1830," and "Apprenticeship Order for Elbert and Everett children of Fanny Artis, October 1834," Apprentice Indentures for Free Negroes (1820–1860), box 2, folder 2, Free Negro and Slave Records, 1754–1860, Southampton County Court Records, Library of Virginia.

26. Daniel W. Crofts, *Old Southampton: Politics and Society in a Virginia County, 1834–1869* (Charlottesville: University of Virginia Press, 1992), 16.

27. Image of 1830 federal manuscript census record for Nathaniel Francis, NARA Record Group 29, microfilm publication M19, reel 196, page 260, accessed at Ancestry.com.

28. Tragle, *The Southampton Slave Revolt of 1831*, 211.

29. Stevenson, *Life in Black and White*, 98–101; Berlin, *Slaves without Masters*, 217–249; Lebsock, *The Free Women of Petersburg*.

30. Ancestry.com. *1830 United States Federal Census* [database on-line], Provo, UT, USA, Ancestry.com Operations, Inc., 2010. Images reproduced by Family Search. Original data: Fifth Census of the United States, 1830 (NARA microfilm publication M19, pages 259–260), Records of the Bureau of the Census, Record Group 29, National Archives, Washington, D.C.

31. Allmendinger, *Nat Turner and the Rising in Southampton County*, 89.

32. Image of 1830 federal manuscript census for Peter Edwards, NARA Record Group 29, microfilm publication M19, reel 196, pages 259–260, accessed on Ancestry.com.

33. Stevenson, *Life in Black and White*, 186–189.

34. King, *Stolen Childhood*, 71–106.

35. Perdue, Barden, and Phillips, *Weevils in the Wheat*, 157.

36. Perdue, Barden, and Phillips, *Weevils in the Wheat*, 281.

37. Perdue, Barden, and Phillips, *Weevils in the Wheat*, 281.

38. Perdue, Barden, and Phillips, *Weevils in the Wheat*, 322. The interviewers attributed the story to Nancy Williams but also noted that they were unsure if she was truly the interviewee who related the story to them. They noted in the interview transcript that "the following story seems at first glance to be an elaboration of a story presented earlier from the typed copy of Nancy Williams's interview in the Va. State Lib. However, the same story is also included in Beverly Jones's Va. State Lib. interview."

39. Perdue, Barden, and Phillips, *Weevils in the Wheat*. None of the enslaved Virginians interviewed by the WPA were born before the Southampton Rebellion. All were children or teens when they were emancipated in 1865.

40. Perdue, Barden, and Phillips, *Weevils in the Wheat*, 75. Crawford's date of birth is listed as 1835. He spent his childhood and young adulthood in Southampton County. Most of his narrative is concerned with his childhood.

41. Virginia officials did not execute any enslaved man named Henry for participating in the Southampton Rebellion. It is possible that Crawford was referring to Hark, whom Joseph Travis enslaved, or Henry, whom Richard Porter enslaved and murdered before he could be captured. For an account of the Black death toll after the rebellion, see Allmendinger, *Nat Turner and the Rising in Southampton County*, 289–300.

42. Perdue, Barden, and Phillips, *Weevils in the Wheat*, 75.

43. Perdue, Barden, and Phillips, *Weevils in the Wheat*, 45.

44. Perdue, Barden, and Phillips, *Weevils in the Wheat*, 162.

45. Perdue, Barden, and Phillips, *Weevils in the Wheat*, 54.

46. Perdue, Barden, and Phillips, *Weevils in the Wheat*, 289.

47. Perdue, Barden, and Phillips, *Weevils in the Wheat*, 289.

48. For events on the Francis farm, see Oates, *The Fires of Jubilee*, 78. See also Allmendinger, *Nat Turner and the Rising in Southampton County*, 78. For the trial records of Nathan, Tom, and Davy, see Tragle, *The Southampton Slave Revolt of 1831*, 190–192, 198–201.

49. Perdue, Barden, and Phillips, *Weevils in the Wheat*, 156.

50. Perdue, Barden, and Phillips, *Weevils in the Wheat*, 294.

51. Perdue, Barden, and Phillips, *Weevils in the Wheat*, 54.

52. Oates, *The Fires of Jubilee*, 77–78; Drewry, *The Southampton Insurrection*, 45–50.

53. Tragle, *The Southampton Slave Revolt of 1831*, 200.

54. Tragle, *The Southampton Slave Revolt of 1831*, 191–193.

55. Allmendinger, *Nat Turner and the Rising in Southampton County*, 223–228. Allmendinger was the first historian to explore the legal inquiry into the origins and plot of the rebellion. He includes profiles of all major witnesses. For more on legal proceedings in antebellum Virginian courts, see Schwarz, *Twice Condemned*; and Philip J. Schwarz, *Slave Laws in Virginia* (Athens: University of Georgia Press, 1996). Patrick Breen offers extensive analysis of the court proceedings in *The Land Shall Be Deluged in Blood*.

56. The court proceedings indicate this using the language "hearing the testimony and the prisoner [by name], assigned counsel." For an example, see Tragle, *The Southampton Slave Revolt of 1831*, 181.

57. Hening, *The New Virginia Justice* (1810 edition), 543. For concise descriptions of proceedings in courts of oyer and terminer, see Turner, *The Confessions of Nat Turner*, 21–22; and Breen, *The Land Shall Be Deluged in Blood*, 107–113.

58. On August 31, 1831, the court ruled that Daniel would be executed on September 5. On September 1, the court set the same execution date for Moses. Tragle, *The Southampton Slave Revolt of 1831*, 179, 185. For the trials of Nathan, Tom, and Davy, see entry for September 6, 1831, Southampton County Court Minute Book, 1830, Southampton County (Va.) County Records Collection, Court Records, reel 34, 93–95.

59. Turner, *The Confessions of Nat Turner*, 97.

60. Tragle, *The Southampton Slave Revolt of 1831*, 200; French, *The Rebellious Slave*, 37–41.

61. Tragle, *The Southampton Slave Revolt of 1831*, 220.

62. Tragle, *The Southampton Slave Revolt of 1831*, 200–201.

63. Tragle, *The Southampton Slave Revolt of 1831*, 196.

64. Tragle, *The Southampton Slave Revolt of 1831*, 196.

65. Tragle, *The Southampton Slave Revolt of 1831*, 196.

66. Tragle, *The Southampton Slave Revolt of 1831*, 196.

67. Tragle, *The Southampton Slave Revolt of 1831*, 200.

68. Tragle, *The Southampton Slave Revolt of 1831*, 200.

69. Tragle, *The Southampton Slave Revolt of 1831*, 200.

70. Tragle, *The Southampton Slave Revolt of 1831*, 200.

71. Hening, *The New Virginia Justice* (1794), 543, 549. According to Virginia law, enslavers were entitled to monetary compensation for enslaved people who were executed or were sold from the state.

72. Camp, *Closer to Freedom*. Camp's concept of competing geographies is particularly useful here: Moses could simultaneously serve and resist those who had hegemonic power.

73. Tragle, *The Southampton Slave Revolt of 1831*, 201.

74. Tragle, *The Southampton Slave Revolt of 1831*, 201.

75. Tragle, *The Southampton Slave Revolt of 1831*, 201.

76. Turner, *The Confessions of Nat Turner*, 38–58. These deaths are listed in Allmendinger, *Nat Turner and the Rising in Southampton County*, 286–288; and Tragle, *The Southampton Slave Revolt of 1831*, 286.

77. Turner, *The Confessions of Nat Turner*, 48–49. See also Allmendinger, *Nat Turner and the Rising in Southampton County*, 102–103 and Appendix A.

78. Both Sam and Dred stood trial, but Will does not appear in court records related to the rebellion. Most historical accounts presume that militia or vigilantes killed him.

79. Turner, *The Confessions of Nat Turner*, 48; Tragle, *The Southampton Slave Revolt of 1831*, 191–192. Allmendinger, who was concerned with connections between white families in the county, also notes that Sam would have been well known in the neighborhood. Allmendinger, *Nat Turner and the Rising in Southampton County*, 90.

80. Tragle, *The Southampton Slave Revolt of 1831*, 201.

81. For a discussion of mercy in Virginia's slave courts, see Schwarz, *Slave Laws in Virginia*.

82. Recent work on what historians call the Second Middle Passage, the internal trade in enslaved property during the antebellum period, has added significantly to our knowledge of the massive shift of white and Black populations from states in the Upper South to the cotton frontier in the Deep South. See Edward E. Baptist, *The Half Has Never Been Told: Slavery and the Making of American Capitalism* (New York: Basic Books, 2014); Walter Johnson, *Soul by Soul: Life inside the Antebellum Slave Market* (Cambridge, MA: Harvard University Press, 1999); Walter Johnson, *River of Dark Dreams: Slavery and Empire in the Cotton Kingdom* (Cambridge, MA: Belknap Press, 2013); and Adam Rothman, *Slave Country: American Expansion and the Origins of the Deep South* (Cambridge, MA: Harvard University Press, 2007).

83. Tragle, *The Southampton Slave Revolt of 1831*, 211.

84. Tragle, *The Southampton Slave Revolt of 1831*, 202–203.

85. Tragle, *The Southampton Slave Revolt of 1831*, 202–203.

86. Allmendinger, *Nat Turner and the Rising in Southampton County*, 296.

87. Tragle, *The Southampton Slave Revolt of 1831*, 200–201.

88. Tragle, *The Southampton Slave Revolt of 1831*, 220.

89. Tragle, *The Southampton Slave Revolt of 1831*, 220.

90. Turner, *The Confessions of Nat Turner*, 96.

91. Tragle, *The Southampton Slave Revolt of 1831*, 220.

92. Turner, *The Confessions of Nat Turner*, 88–93.

93. Perdue, Barden, and Phillips, *Weevils in the Wheat*, 75.

94. Perdue, Barden, and Phillips, *Weevils in the Wheat*, 67. Cornelia Carney was born in 1836.

Chapter 5. Surviving Southampton

1. Allmendinger, *Nat Turner and the Rising in Southampton County*, Appendix F.

2. For the persistent emotional distress within the white community, see Parramore, *Southampton County, Virginia*, 116–119; and Allmendinger, *Nat Turner and the Rising in Southampton County*, 261–265.

3. Turner, *The Confessions of Nat Turner*, 38–58; Allmendinger, *Nat Turner and the Rising in Southampton County*, 286–288; Tragle, *The Southampton Slave Revolt of 1831*, 286.

4. In her study of local law in the early national and antebellum Carolinas, Laura Edwards defines it as "a hierarchical order that forced everyone into its patriarchal embrace and raised collective interests over those of any given individual." This understanding of local law best characterizes the legal practices of Southampton County's magistrates and the broader community that assembled, by choice and by force, in Jerusalem after the rebellion. See Edwards, *The People and Their Peace*, 7.

5. The full title of Gray's publication was *The Confessions of Nat Turner, the Leader of the Late Insurrection in Southampton, Va.: As Fully and Voluntarily Made to Thomas R. Gray, in the Prison Where He Was Confined, and Acknowledged by Him to Be Such When Read before the Court of Southampton, with the Certificate, under the Seal of the Court Convened at Jerusalem, Nov. 5, 1831, for His Trial. Also an Authentic Account of the Whole Insurrection, with Lists of the Whites Who Were Murdered and of the Negroes Brought before the Court of Southampton, and There Sentenced, &c*. See Turner, *The Confessions of Nat Turner*, 38.

6. Scot French's extensive study of Nat Turner in historical memory and American culture is particularly useful for understanding how Turner changed in public memory from an individual community member to an archetype of mythical status. French, *The Rebellious Slave*.

7. Turner, *The Confessions of Nat Turner*, 38–43.

8. Turner, *The Confessions of Nat Turner*, 40.

9. For more about the writing and production of *The Confessions of Nat Turner*, see David F. Allmendinger Jr., "The Construction of *The Confessions of Nat Turner*," in Greenberg, *Nat Turner*, 24–44.

10. Anthony E. Kaye, "Neighborhoods and Nat Turner: The Making of a Slave Rebel and the Unmaking of a Slave Rebellion," *Journal of the Early Republic* 27, no. 4 (2007): 705–720.

11. Patrick Breen, "A Prophet in His Own Land: Support for Nat Turner and His Rebellion within Southampton's Black Community," in Greenberg, *Nat Turner*, 103–119.

12. Turner, *The Confessions of Nat Turner*, 43.

13. It is true that he also said that his community did not always agree with him or his theology. See Breen, "A Prophet in His Own Land," 103–118.

14. Turner, *The Confessions of Nat Turner*, 51.

15. Sylviane Diouf offers an excellent analysis of African American truancy practices in Southside Virginia and all over the antebellum South. See Diouf, *Slavery's Exiles*.

16. Turner, *The Confessions of Nat Turner*, 51.

17. As in many colonial contexts, the earliest courts in the county were convened in residents' houses or in central public places. In 1752, Southampton County residents built their first courthouse. After it was destroyed by fire, they rebuilt it in 1767. In fact, Jerusalem's original name was Southampton Court House. Jerusalem (now Courtland) continues to use the brick courthouse completed in 1834. Parramore, *Southampton County, Virginia*, 29–30, 47. See also "Court Systems," Southampton County Virginia, https://www.southamptoncounty.org/departments/court_systems/index.php.

18. Edwards, *The People and Their Peace*, 75–77. Parramore, *Southampton County, Virginia*, 186.

19. Breen, *The Land Shall Be Deluged in Blood*, 110.

20. Breen, *The Land Shall Be Deluged in Blood*, 108–110.

21. Edwards, *The People and Their Peace*, 7.

22. Breen, *The Land Shall Be Deluged in Blood*, 108–111.

23. Allmendinger, *Nat Turner and the Rising in Southampton County*, 223–224.

24. Tragle, *The Southampton Revolt of 1831*, 198.

25. William C. Parker, James L. French, Thomas R. Gray, William B. Boyle, and Robert Burchett served as counsels for enslaved defendants. See Allmendinger, *Nat Turner and the Rising in Southampton County*, 270–279; and Tragle, *The Southampton Slave Revolt of 1831*, 229–245.

26. Meriwether Broadnax served as the prosecutor. He was the brother of General William Broadnax, who had participated in the militia effort to put down the rebellion. Broadnax deposed witnesses to build cases against enslaved defendants. For more on his work and life, see Allmendinger, *Nat Turner and the Rising in Southampton County*, 229, 273.

27. Court minutes were signed and approved by a justice who presided during each trial. The county clerk, James Rochelle, was responsible for recording court proceedings and making sure they were dispatched to the governor for review. See Allmendinger, *Nat Turner and the Rising in Southampton County*, 159; Breen,

The Land Shall Be Deluged in Blood, 14–15; and Tragle, *The Southampton Slave Revolt of 1831*, 173–177.

28. The great majority of justices ruled in favor of the commonwealth and sentenced defendants to death. However, they asked the governor for leniency in many cases. The actual number of those the sheriff executed was thus eighteen. Allmendinger, *Nat Turner and the Rising in Southampton County*, 291.

29. Edwards, *The People and Their Peace*, 3; Kirt von Daacke, *Freedom Has a Face: Race, Identity, and Community in Jefferson's Virginia* (Charlottesville: University of Virginia Press), 3–5.

30. Tragle, *The Southampton Revolt of 1831*, 177–179.

31. Edwards, *The People and Their Peace*, 109.

32. Hadden, *Slave Patrols*, 72–77. Hadden explicates the cross-class relations between white men who served in militias and slave patrols in antebellum Virginia, noting that the militia and patrols allowed middling white men to participate in the power structure that governed Black residents.

33. Edwards, *The People and Their Peace*, 200–201. In the 1820s and 1830s, courts prioritized preserving local relationships and hierarchies. Slavery, the bedrock of social hierarchy in the early antebellum South, was a variable institution made in the image of "localized dynamics of subordination." This does not mean that slavery was benign or humane; it only means that those in power adapted it over time to suit their needs. This did not translate into rights or precedents because legal practice was so localized.

34. Allmendinger, *Nat Turner and the Rising in Southampton County*, 87–214.

35. Tragle, *The Southampton Revolt of 1831*, 177; trial of Daniel, August 31, 1831, Southampton County Court Minute Book, reel 34, page 72.

36. Tragle, *The Southampton Revolt of 1831*, 179. Tragle used backslashes to indicate line breaks in the original documents.

37. Tragle, *The Southampton Revolt of 1831*, 178.

38. Tragle, *The Southampton Revolt of 1831*, 178.

39. Image of 1830 federal manuscript census record for Richard Porter, NARA Record Group 29, microfilm M19, roll 196, pages 256–257, accessed on Ancestry.com. For a photo of Porter's house, see Tragle, *The Southampton Slave Revolt of 1831*, 163. See also Drewry, *The Southampton Insurrection*, 49.

40. Tragle, *The Southampton Slave Revolt of 1831*, 176.

41. Tragle, *The Southampton Slave Revolt of 1831*, 176.

42. Tragle, *The Southampton Slave Revolt of 1831*, 179.

43. Tragle, *The Southampton Slave Revolt of 1831*, 232–237.

44. Tragle, *The Southampton Slave Revolt of 1831*, 217–219.

45. Tragle, *The Southampton Slave Revolt of 1831*, 193.

46. Tragle, *The Southampton Slave Revolt of 1831*, 208.

47. Breen points out that the court and the prosecutor in particular seem to have afforded defendants a type of common-law Fifth Amendment that did not require them to testify against themselves. Breen, *The Land Shall Be Deluged in Blood*, 107–138.

48. Entries for August 31–November 21, 1831, County Court Minute Books, pages 72–143, reel 34.

49. Other scholars have taken this to mean that African American women did not support the rebellion and actively worked against it. I argue that they had little or no power to refuse to testify, but they did have the ability to omit details from their testimony. See Mary Kemp Davis, "'What Happened in This Place?': In Search of the Female Slave in the Nat Turner Slave Insurrection," in Greenberg, *Nat Turner,* 162–178.

50. The prosecution used witnesses fifty-nine times. The defense did so only thirteen times. Tragle, *The Southampton Slave Revolt of 1831;* entries for August 31–November 21, 1831, County Court Minute Books.

51. Tragle, *The Southampton Slave Revolt of 1831,* 185.

52. Tragle, *The Southampton Slave Revolt of 1831,* 185.

53. Schwarz, *Twice Condemned,* 35–58. Schwarz uses the term "criminal slaves" and notes that the legal documents of the time used the term. For his discussion of the Southampton Rebellion, see 234–235.

54. Tragle, *The Southampton Slave Revolt of 1831,* 185.

55. Entry for September 1, 1831, County Court Minute Book, pages 74–76, reel 34; Tragle, *The Southampton Slave Revolt of 1831,* 179–182.

56. Tragle, *The Southampton Slave Revolt of 1831,* 183.

57. Tragle, *The Southampton Slave Revolt of 1831,* 183.

58. Allmendinger, *Nat Turner and the Rising in Southampton County,* 125–129.

59. Tragle, *The Southampton Slave Revolt of 1831,* 183.

60. Tragle, *The Southampton Slave Revolt of 1831,* 183.

61. Tragle, *The Southampton Slave Revolt of 1831,* 74–75.

62. Tragle, *The Southampton Slave Revolt of 1831,* 74.

63. Tragle, *The Southampton Slave Revolt of 1831,* 183.

64. Tragle, *The Southampton Slave Revolt of 1831,* 183.

65. Tragle, *The Southampton Slave Revolt of 1831,* 183.

66. Tragle, *The Southampton Slave Revolt of 1831,* 182–184.

67. Tragle, *The Southampton Slave Revolt of 1831,* 194–195.

68. Allmendinger, *Nat Turner and the Rising in Southampton County,* 187.

69. Tragle, *The Southampton Slave Revolt of 1831,* 194–195.

70. Tragle, *The Southampton Slave Revolt of 1831,* 194–195.

71. Drewry, *The Southampton Insurrection,* 60. Drewry's account states that Nealson helped himself to "dinner then preparing" and refers to Cynthia as "the cook."

72. "Constitutional Whig, September 26, 1831," quoted in Turner, *The Confessions of Nat Turner,* 81. In an anonymous letter dated September 17, 1831, that Greenberg attributes to Thomas R. Gray, a local Jerusalem resident gave an account of the rebellion and noted the beating of Turner's wife and her surrender of the papers. The letter is one of the very few references on record to Nat Turner's wife, Cherry. For details about the very few threads about Cherry Turner in extant records of enslavers, see Allmendinger, *Nat Turner and the Rising in Southampton County,* 63–67.

73. Allmendinger, *Nat Turner and the Rising in Southampton County*, 182; Tragle, *The Southampton Slave Revolt of 1831*, 208–209.

74. Tragle, *The Southampton Slave Revolt of 1831*, 213–216. David Allmendinger's careful research of property transfers between whites in the county also connects Beck to the transfers among the Vaughn, Barrow, and Parker families. As enslaved people circulated, so did their connections to kin on other farms. Beck was embedded in such a community. See Allmendinger, *Nat Turner and the Rising in Southampton County*, 156.

75. Tragle, *The Southampton Slave Revolt of 1831*, 227.

76. There were limits to the hysteria, however. Many whites chose to assess local populations of free Black people based on long-standing relationships with them and their useful contributions to the community. For example, Kirt von Daacke writes that "even after the bloody Nat Turner Rebellion in Southampton County in 1831, Albemarle did not dramatically change its maintenance of racial hierarchy. Free people of color were not rounded up and charged with violating removal law." Von Daacke, *Freedom Has a Face*, 80. See also Ely, *Israel on the Appomattox*, 175–186.

77. Turner, *The Confessions of Nat Turner*, 21; Tragle, *The Southampton Slave Revolt of 1831*, 175.

78. Hening, *The New Virginia Justice* (1794), 436.

79. Hening, *The New Virginia Justice* (1794), 548.

80. The penal code stipulated that county courts could examine and indict free persons, including free people of color. However, county magistrates needed to send such cases to a higher court for trial. Hening, *The New Virginia Justice* (1794), 205, 207.

81. Tragle, *The Southampton Slave Revolt of 1831*, 202.

82. Tragle, *The Southampton Slave Revolt of 1831*, 203.

83. Tragle, *The Southampton Slave Revolt of 1831*, 202–203.

84. Tragle, *The Southampton Slave Revolt of 1831*, 203.

85. Tragle, *The Southampton Slave Revolt of 1831*, 203.

86. Tragle, *The Southampton Slave Revolt of 1831*, 185.

87. Tragle, *The Southampton Slave Revolt of 1831*, 202–203.

88. Tragle, *The Southampton Slave Revolt of 1831*, 223–227.

89. Breen, *The Land Shall Be Deluged in Blood*, 131–132.

90. The state's legal code had long included statutes that sought to expel free Black people and govern the nature of their freedom. See Hening, *The New Virginia Justice* (1794), 539–554; and von Daacke, *Freedom Has a Face*, 1–43.

91. The Virginia law that required free people of color to register with local officials was enacted in 1793. A removal law followed in 1806. The adherence to these laws was spotty and very locally contingent. See von Daacke, *Freedom Has a Face*, 71, 77–79, 113, 159; and Hening, *The New Virginia Justice* (1794), 546.

92. I do not have a complete count of registrations in court minute books. However, specific registries that are separate from the county minute books are archived at the Library of Virginia. See Southampton County (Va.) Free Negro and

Slave Records, 1754–1860, reel 90, Southampton County Court Records, Library of Virginia, Richmond.

93. A record of residency was important for all free people, Black and white, across the United States in the antebellum period. For more on vagrancy and poor laws, see Ruth Wallis Herndon, *Unwelcome Americans: Living on the Margin in Early New England* (Philadelphia: University of Pennsylvania Press, 2001); and Seth Rockman, *Scraping By: Wage Labor, Slavery, and Survival in Early Baltimore* (Baltimore, MD: Johns Hopkins University Press, 2009).

94. Free people of color lived under many repressive laws that constrained their mobility. Their residence in white households throughout the county also placed them under the same surveillance as enslaved people. Also, slave patrols were instructed and required by law to police both enslaved people and free people of color. A substantial list of registrants appeared in the local record at the end of 1831. "List of Free Negroes, December 1831," Free Negro Lists, 1801–1831, Free Negro and Slave Records, 1754–1860, box 2, folder 2, Library of Virginia, Richmond. See also Berlin, *Slaves without Masters*; and Hadden, *Slave Patrols*. See also Slave Patrol Records, Southampton County (Va.) Free Negro and Slave Records, 1754–1860, reel 90, Southampton County Court Records, Library of Virginia, Richmond.

95. The court did not try anyone in connection with the rebellion between September 28 and October 17. County Court Minute Books, September and October, 1831, pages 114–119, reel 34.

96. Allmendinger, *Nat Turner and the Rising in Southampton County*, 240; Parramore, *Southampton County, Virginia*, 108; Turner, *The Confessions of Nat Turner*, 53.

97. Entry for October 17, 1831, County Court Minute Book, page 114, reel 34.

98. Allmendinger, *Nat Turner and the Rising in Southampton County*, 231; Tragle, *The Southampton Slave Revolt of 1831*, 242; entry for October 17, 1831, County Court Minute Book, page 114, reel 34.

99. Entry for October 17, 1831, County Court Minute Book, page 116, reel 34.

100. Entry for October 17, 1831, County Court Minute Book, page 116, reel 34.

101. Entry for October 18, 1831, County Court Minute Book, page 120, reel 34.

102. Entry for October 18, 1831, County Court Minute Book, pages 119–121, reel 34.

103. Entries for November 24 and December 19, 1831, County Court Minute Book, pages 136 and 143, reel 34. Maneriva Drew, John R. Bailey, and William Brown registered on November 24, 1831. And on December 19, David Ricks received replacement registration papers and Gabriel Ricks, Mary Artist, Hubbard Artist, and Cathy Crocker registered.

104. The names Artis or Artist, Ricks, and Whitfield all appear frequently in free negro registries. Free People of Color Registry, Southampton County (Va.) Free Negro and Slave Records, 1754–1860, reel 90, Southampton County Court Records, Library of Virginia, Richmond.

105. Apprenticeship was common throughout the United States. In New England, serving an apprenticeship could grant an inhabitant legal residency that

could protect them from the practice of warning out. See Herndon, *Unwelcome Americans*, 5; Hening, *The New Virginia Justice* (1794), 66–68.

106. Berlin, *Slaves without Masters*.

107. John Floyd, *Niles' Weekly Register*, January 7, 1832, 350–351.

108. For example, on November 21, 1831, David and Diddy Byrd indentured five of their children, Diddy, Nancy, Henry, Anne, and Jane, to Benjamin Whitfield. Whitfield included only free people of color in his household in 1830 and owned no enslaved people. He is also recorded as the former enslaver of a number of free people of color in the free Negro and slave records for Southampton County. This indenture of a group of siblings kept them together and housed them with an apparently sympathetic white landowner. At the end of months of upheaval resulting from the rebellion, this makes sense as a strategy for free parents who were anxious to keep their children close. Southampton County (Va.) Free Negro and Slave Records, 1754–1860, reel 90, Southampton County Court Records, Library of Virginia, Richmond. See also Hening, *The New Virginia Justice* (1794), 63–66; and image of 1830 federal manuscript census record for David Byrd, from NARA Record Group 29, microfilm M19, reel 196, page 246, accessed on Ancestry.com.

109. List of Free Negroes, St. Luke's Parish, 1822, Southampton County (Va.) Free Negro and Slave Records, 1754–1860, Southampton County Court Records, reel 90, Library of Virginia, Richmond.

110. Indenture of Diddy, Nancy, Henry, Anne, and Jane Byrd to Benjamin Whitfield.

111. Benjamin Whitfield freed a number of enslaved people in his will, resulting in the appearance of almost thirty free people of color in free Negro records for the county. Some of his descendants, which did not include the Benjamin Whitfield mentioned here in 1831, fought his will and petitioned for a reversal of the emancipation of their relative's property. See Petition 21679904, June 1799, Race and Slavery Petitions Project, https://library.uncg.edu/slavery/petitions/details.aspx?pid=14444. In the 1810s and 1820s, Benjamin Whitfield owned a single enslaved person. But by 1830, Whitfield no longer held anyone in bondage. Image of 1830 federal census record for Benjamin Whitfield, NARA Record Group 29, microfilm publication M19, reel 196, page 246, accessed on Ancestry.com.

112. Free Negro and Slave Records, Indenture for Boyd Whitfield, Southampton County (Va.) Free Negro and Slave Records, 1754–1860, Southampton County Court Records, Library of Virginia, Richmond; image of Federal Census records for William W. Cutler for 1820 (pages 219–220) and 1830 (pages 253–254), *1820 Census and 1830 United States Federal Census* [database online]. Provo, UT, USA: Ancestry.com Operations, 2010. Images reproduced by Family Search.

113. The slaveholding that Reuben Whitfield, Jacob Underwood, and Jacob Bailey petitioned the court for included twenty-seven slaves. Some may have chosen to leave the county after they were emancipated. Petition 21679904, accessed via https://library.uncg.edu/slavery/petitions/details.aspx?pid=14444.

114. Indenture of John Artis to Samuel Story, January 16, 1832, Apprentice Indentures, 1820–1860, Free Negro and Slave Records, 1754–1860, box 2, folder 2, Southampton County Court Records, Library of Virginia, Richmond.

115. The 1820 census (where Story's first name is spelled Zaceus rather than Zacheus) lists no slaves and five free people of color in Story's household. Image of 1820 federal manuscript census record for Samuel Story, NARA Record Group 29, microfilm publication M33, reel 142, pages 241–242, accessed on Ancestry.com; image of 1830 federal manuscript census record for Samuel Story, NARA Record Group 29, microfilm publication M19, reel 196, pages 247–248; indenture of Jack E. Turner and Josiah Turner to Zacheus Story, February 14, 1832, Free Negro and Slave Records, 1754–1860, box 2, folder 2, Southampton County Court Records, Library of Virginia, Richmond.

116. Irons, *The Origins of Proslavery Christianity*, 150–151.

117. Image of 1840 federal manuscript census record for Benjamin Whitfield, NARA Record Group 29, microfilm publication M704, reel 575, pages 114–115, accessed on Ancestry.com; Parramore, *Southampton County, Virginia*, 114–115.

118. Perdue, Barden, and Phillips, *Weevils in the Wheat*, 67.

119. Perdue, Barden, and Phillips, *Weevils in the Wheat*, 299.

Conclusion

1. Andrew Lind, "Road Name Change Proposed," *Tidewater News*, August 7, 2015, accessed August 7, 2015, https://www.thetidewaternews.com/2015/08/07/road-name-change-proposed/.

2. Alfred L. Brophy, "Why Northerners Should Support Conferederate [*sic*] Monuments," *Washington Post*, July 14, 2015, https://www.washingtonpost.com/posteverything/wp/2015/07/14/why-northerners-should-support-the-preservation-of-conferederate-monuments/.

3. Drewry, *The Southampton Insurrection*, 52.

4. Turner, *The Confessions of Nat Turner*.

5. Lind, "Road Name Change Proposed."

6. "Descendants Offer His Hiding Place to Be Part of Driving Tour," *Tidewater News*, February 10, 2011, http://www.thetidewaternews.com/2011/02/10/nat-turner%E2%80%99s-descendants-offer-his-hiding-place-to-be-part-of-driving-tour/.

7. Greenberg published an anonymous letter that noted that whites beat her to coerce her to surrender some papers; see Turner, *The Confessions of Nat Turner*, 81. Allmendinger provides a careful look at the sources of white enslavers that might include Cherry; see Allmendinger, *Nat Turner and the Rising in Southampton County*, 63–67. In the 1940s, Lucy Mae Turner and Fannie V. Turner, two descendants of Nat and Cherry Turner, published an account that traced their family history. Their article has no footnotes and they do not name Cherry Turner, but they would have had access to oral history. They argue that enslaved people were

not docile and that their ancestor's rebellion fell within a continuum of resistance. Lucy Mae Turner and Fannie V. Turner, "The Story of Nat Turner's Descendants," *Negro History Bulletin* 10, no. 7 (1947): 155–65. Lucy Mae Turner published about her family again in 1955 in an article in which she referred to her grandmother as Fannie, not Cherry. Lucy Mae Turner, "The Family of Nat Turner, 1831 to 1954," *Negro History Bulletin* 18, no. 7 (1955): 155–58. Lucy Mae Turner was a keeper of Black history, an active participant in the Black freedom struggle, and a candidate for justice of the peace in East St. Louis, Illinois. Lucy Mae Turner and E. Imogene Wilson, "Kin of Nat Turner," *Negro History Bulletin* 27, no. 4 (1964): 78.

8. "Nat Turner's Descendants Offer His Hiding Place to Be Part of Driving Tour," *Tidewater News*, February 10, 2011, https://www.thetidewaternews.com/2011/02/10/nat-turner%E2%80%99s-descendants-offer-his-hiding-place-to-be-part-of-driving-tour/.

Index

VANESSA M. HOLDEN is an assistant professor of
history at the University of Kentucky.

Women, Gender, and Sexuality in American History

All Our Trials: Prisons, Policing, and the Feminist Fight to End Violence
   Emily L. Thuma
Sophonisba Breckinridge: Championing Women's Activism in Modern
   America   *Anya Jabour*
Starring Women: Celebrity, Patriarchy, and American Theater, 1790–1850
   Sara E. Lampert
Surviving Southampton: African American Women and Resistance in Nat Turner's
   Community   *Vanessa M. Holden*

The University of Illinois Press
is a founding member of the
Association of University Presses.

_____

Composed in 10.25/14 Chaparral Pro
with Plantin Std display
by Lisa Connery
at the University of Illinois Press
Manufactured by Sheridan Books, Inc.

University of Illinois Press
1325 South Oak Street
Champaign, IL 61820-6903
www.press.uillinois.edu